SANDI BROWN

KNOWN

A Daughter's Search for a Killer, Her Identity, and the Heart of God

KNOWN: A Daughter's Search for a Killer, Her Identity, and the Heart of God
Copyright © 2020 by Sandra Rohrer.

All rights reserved.

This book is protected by the copyright laws of the United States of America. This book may not be copied or reprinted for commercial gain or profit. The use of short quotations or occasional page copying for personal or group study is permitted and encouraged. Permission will be granted upon request. Unless others identified.

Scripture quotations marked TPT are from The Passion Translation®. Copyright © 2017, 2018 by Passion & Fire Ministries, Inc. Used by permission. All rights reserved. ThePassionTranslation.com.

All Scripture quotations are from The Passion Translation®. Copyright © 2017, 2018 by Passion & Fire Ministries, Inc. Used by permission. All rights reserved.

Cover Art: © Jill Dolan www.jillmarieart.weebly.com
Interior & Exterior Design: © Paula Hays www.floraliescreative.com

Printed in the United States of America
www.sandrarohrer.com

PDF (Paperback) ISBN10: 1-949494-10-1
ISBN13: 978-1-949494-10-5

***Some names have been changed in this book.

Subscribe to Sandra's mailing list to have access to exclusive photos & content, and future KNOWN Merch at www.sandrarohrer.com

Follow Sandra on IG @sandraroars

To my family—
You are *always* loved

Table of Contents

Introduction	vii

The Questions

Artist	13
Are You Here?	17
Do You Hear Me?	27
Do You Create Tragedy?	41
Can You Redeem My Life?	53
Can You Heal My Heart?	69
Can I Have My Own Family?	75

The Facets

Tear Collector	91
Wall Shaker	103
Weaver	121
Baggage Taker	129
Adventurer	143
Territory Taker	157
Healer	171
Wild Dreamer	181
Beautiful One	189
Jeweler	201
Gardener	213
Compass	225
Daring Hope	241

Father *251*
The Great Invitation *273*
Acknowledgements *275*

INTRODUCTION

"God, I want to know You so well that when I die, I will not be surprised by who You are."

I was driving down a country road in Iowa when I had this notable thought. My heart yearned deeply to know Him like never before. I heard the impossibility of this statement, yet He heard a prayer— and He answered. My favorite Bible verse is John 17:3 in The Passion Translation (TPT).

"Eternal life means to know and experience You as the only true God, and to know and experience Jesus Christ, as the Son whom You have sent."

Yes, He would introduce me to Himself and I would experience His many Facets in an unexpected way: through two haunting mysteries and excruciating pain.

As a young Christian, I read the Letters (from here on I will refer to the Bible as the Letters) and saw Father God's provision for His children to walk in freedom. I saw His desire for me to have an abundant life, yet my broken heart was bonded to pain. I was missing the heart-wholeness I read about in the Letters. An invisible chasm loomed between what I believed and the life I was living.

I needed an encounter of His love after years of heartache and neglect. I asked God for the baptism of His love. I received it! I immediately felt a supernatural peace come over me as I slumped over on a sofa, overwhelmed by it. Shortly after that, I read John 16:5-16. There it was. Holy Spirit is the Comforter, Helper, Divine Encourager, and my Advocate. He is a person.

Jesus said, "But after I depart, I will send Him to you…But when the truth-giving Spirit comes, He will unveil the reality of every truth within you. He won't speak His own message, but only what He hears from the Father, and He will reveal prophetically to you what is to come. He will glorify me on the earth, for He will receive from me what is mine and reveal it to you. He will guide you to all truth." In that moment, I heard the Holy Spirit speak to me for the first time.

You are not alone. I am with you.

Holy Spirit whispered inside my heart! With delight, I shared the story with a friend. This was my first conversation with God and the beginning of my real relationship with Him.

Nothing has shifted my life more than communicating with Father God, Jesus, and Holy Spirit. We have an intimate relationship. I speak, He listens. He speaks, I listen. I ask questions, He answers, and poses questions back to me. He speaks to me in so many ways. He gives me pictures in my mind's eye. He visits my night's dreams, He brings up the number 613 (my birthday) or 717 (more on that later), and of course, He shares His Letters.

One of the most significant conversations I had with Him was when He answered my prayer to know Him deeply.

I want to take you to the Other Side. You have been through so much, Dear Heart, and I want to heal your heart by showing you the facets of Mine.

"I'm ready! Let's go! I want to discover the beautiful facets of Your heart!"

Known is my invitation to you to discover them along with me. The Tear Collector, Wall Shaker, Weaver, Baggage Taker, Adventurer, Territory Taker, Healer, Wild Dreamer, Beautiful One, Jeweler, Gardener, My Compass, Daring Hope, and Father are the different facets of the Heart of God that I now know through intimate dialogue, looming mysteries, and traumatic pain.

These are the facets of God that not only solved the mysteries that left me broken, but brought a healing balm to my soul. He did what I thought was impossible; He answered my questions and healed my heart!

I pray my story becomes a springboard for you to experience and know the many facets of His heart.

— Sandra

Note to the Reader

This story is a tapestry of my real-life experiences along with scenes that paint a picture of my encounters with God. These scenes are representative of many real and intimate conversations I've had with Him. They were crafted to display to you, the reader, my perceptions of His heart, His voice, and His perspective on the tragedies and triumphs I've endured. I've woven together both truth and artistic storytelling to make my memoir a journey for the reader – a journey to encounter the Facets of God's heart.

Part One

The Questions

Chapter 1

ARTIST

*…When You create me in the secret place – carefully,
skillfully shaping me from nothing to something, You saw
who You created me to be, before I became me!*

~ *Psalm 139:15-16 TPT*

Before the foundation of time, peeling back the jewel filled curtain, the guardian peers into the creation room. Her eyes land on the Artist. She watches the Artist's eyes reflect light and
delight, as He rolls the scroll out for Sandra. It is time to design His daughter. The Artist's eyes jump from the scroll to the clay. He moves the clay with precision, intention, and purpose. With a brush stroke, the Artist encircles Sandra with the light of His heart. Each adorning stroke has no beginning and no end.

The Artist's heart holds a plethora of virtues and desires, He blows on each one making them dance and come alive. With enjoyment, He places each one in the core of her heart. He smiles while creating her heart. His tears add to the clay as His heart hovers over His beautiful creation. Bright waves of love crash through the Artist's heart through the brush. Waves of love cascade and encapsulate His daughter. An intoxicating fragrance of orange blossom and white lilies fill the inner hiding place.

Looking to His right, He pulls a book from the shelf. On the cover, He writes her name, Sandra, and begins to write her story.

The Artist decrees with His pen, declaring victory with each virtue:

> *Sandra, you will know Me and experience My love for you.*
> *Sandra, you will extend mercy to those who don't deserve it.*
> *Sandra, kindness will follow you each and every day. You will be kind.*
> *Sandra, you will persevere. You will be rewarded for your endurance.*
> *Sandra, you are creative. You have access to all the creativity I have.*
> *Sandra, you will walk where brave people are afraid to walk because you are full of courage.*
> *Sandra, you will love extravagantly. Fear will not be your comforter.*
> *Sandra, you have a strong voice. You will make a mark in the world.*
> *Sandra, you are whole. You will draw others to My heart and into wholeness.*

When each promise leaves the Artist's lips, they transform into dream seeds planted within her heart. The Artist closes the book and finishes designing Sandra's heart, locking it with a key forged in gold. An intricate crown is etched deep within the key. This key was crafted by the Artist and it unlocks His heart, too.

The Artist summons the guardian to draw close. He hands her the sacred key. Her giant feathered wings drape down her back.

The Artist confides in the guardian,

She will go through many difficulties on earth, but when she discovers My heart she will understand who I created her to be. I will reveal My love and purpose for her on her journey. She will be a carrier of healing and hope. Please keep a watchful eye on her.

The guardian nods her head, opens her breastplate, and places the key near her heart.

Sandra never knew the meticulous written details and timing forged to create her. The Artist places mercy, kindness, and perseverance into her being. With love and audacious joy, He adds fun, beauty, adventure, dreams, daring hope, and "the impossible can be possible" attitude. The Artist handpicks and places these things into her soul and closes her heart.

Chapter 2

ARE YOU HERE?

I am with you, and will watch over you, wherever you go.
~Genesis 28:15

I don't know what to do. I feel a heaviness. I feel empty. Today, treasured life was taken from me. I have heard about You, but I do not know You. Are You here? I have all of these questions stirring within me, and my mind is struggling to make sense of it all.
I want to share my heart. I want to understand the loss and pain I endured as this tragic event unfolded. Loss is a little word, yet it carries such majestic emptiness. The four letters seem so insignificant and I feel like I'm dying inside. Will You listen to my words of suffering and loss? Will You collect my pool of tears?

The phone rings, 4:00am flashes on the clock.

"Sandy?" The voice of Roy, my stepdad says urgently, "I'm coming over!"

"What is going on?" I wonder why he is calling so early. He abruptly hangs up the phone and drives across town to the house where I'm babysitting. I pace the linoleum floor, fearfully expecting his arrival. Who is hurt? Did someone die?

What happened?

I stare at my left hand. I recollect the moments just days before, visiting my mother's home in Iowa City, showing her my new prized possession, a thin gold band with a small diamond on top. Wesley and I are engaged.

Are You here? Do You see me rushing to the stairs to answer the door? Do You see Roy leading me to the living room to share the horror?

"Your mom died in a car fire," Roy whispers with tears rolling down his face.

Do You see me buckling to the carpet?

As I fall to the sea-foam green carpet, I want it to carry me to the ocean. Everything around me is silent as I feel the piercing pain through my heart. My fist hammers the ground.

I scream, "No! No! No!"

Lost in my own world of distress I become aware of Joy. The little girl I'm babysitting gathers herself in a ball. She cradles her legs on the sofa, watching me suffer. My hysteria awakened her. I don't want her here, but I don't have the strength to tell her to leave. It's a private moment, like when an animal hides to die—my heart is dying, and I want to be alone.

Even in shock, I need answers. I call my mom's landline. Jerry, my mom's ex-boyfriend, answers.

"Jerry?" My brows furrow.

"Yes, it's Daddy," he confidently replies.

Who does he think he is? Why is he answering the phone, 'It's Daddy?' He is my twin sisters' father, but not my father. I've only met him a handful of times, I barely know him. Besides, everything is far from okay; I feel physically and emotionally abandoned. My soul is destitute. My mother is dead.

"What happened?" I wonder.

"Here, talk to Barb." Jerry hands the phone to my aunt. My mom's sister, Barb is on the phone, "The accident happened last night when your mom left to get Jerry ice cream."

"Ice Cream? She left to get him ice cream?!" I repeat. This is odd. I don't understand.

"Come to your mom's trailer," she demands.

"Alright, we'll be there soon."

Do You realize, like I do, the identity of my biological father just died with my mother? How will I ever find him?

In a moment I've become an orphan.

Are You with me as I drive to my mom's home?

I ride with Roy and my teenage brother, Jason, to her trailer in Iowa City. The 25-minute drive is painfully long. I can't believe the emptiness I feel. A thousand thoughts flood my mind. I will never talk to her again. I want to arrive quickly so I can experience her absence for myself. Is this really true? Is this really my reality? Is she really gone? Will I never talk to her again? All of these questions whirl in my mind.

We pull into the Regency Trailer Court and turn on Apache Trail.

Familiar vehicles from my mom's family line the sides of the street.

She died a quarter of a mile away. The family decides to gather at her home first before going to the accident scene. We aren't sure if her death is an accident or suicide. A few years ago, my mom attempted suicide and it was too early to rule out any cause of death.

My mom's family and her ex-boyfriend's family fill the small trailer. The smell of stale smoke permeates the living room. I survey the room, scanning faces. Aunt Fern, Aunt Barb, Uncle Tony, and my cousins sit in the living room. Barb comforts herself by rubbing her belly. She is pregnant with twin girls. My younger cousins are quiet, their heads down staring at the calico carpet in disbelief. Barb increases the tension with a telling outburst, "Sue would not leave the girls to get you ice cream!"

This makes me cringe inside. I hate confrontation and her accusing Jerry of lying makes me uncomfortable, so I sit quiet, too.

My eyes land on Jerry, my mom's ex-boyfriend and the father of her sixteen-month-old twin daughters. "Why is he even here?" I angrily think to myself. He has little involvement in the twins' lives, but here he sits looking smug. Jerry's beady blue eyes hide behind steel frame glasses. I notice one ear seems higher than the other, I wonder what she saw in him. His sister,
Melanie, is here too, sitting next to him. To my knowledge, Jerry's half-brother is the only other family member who met the twins. Everyone else in his family is MIA.

I'm surprised to see Melanie; this is the first time she is meeting the girls. Her bulging eyes dart back and forth across the room, hiding behind her oversize glasses. The two of them sit on the pink-and-blue futon in the living room, avoiding the rest of the family.

In the kitchen, Roy is standing with arms folded and a scowl on his face. My brother Jason, with disbelief in his eyes, stands beside him.

I learn the police arrived at Roy's house earlier that morning to relay the news of my mom's death. He's concerned with sharing the news with us. He's worried how we will handle it. As he's standing there, I can see Roy's frustration. The mother of his kids, the wife of his youth, gone. Roy is a fixer; a peacekeeper, and this is something he can't fix. For Roy, this isn't the time for him to grieve, it's time to help his children navigate this tragedy.

My mom's trailer is overtaken with confusion, disbelief, sadness, and anger. Then, disheveled Pam shows up. I'm wondering why she is here. Pam is my mom's cousin, who lives down the street. Her trailer is full of foster kids and dogs. She brings her stress from her house to my mom's house.

I just want everyone to leave. I want to be alone. This isn't some kind of family reunion. I stand in the kitchen overlooking the living room, feeling sick to my stomach. I can't believe she is gone. How will I live without my mother? Fear bombards my thoughts, I hope she didn't intentionally hurt herself.

Do You know what happened last night? Were You with my mom?

My Aunt Barb raises her voice with Jerry and Melanie. Barb notices the phone cord is broken, leaving part of its clear plastic stuck in the phone. "What happened to this?" Her voice escalates.

    I can't take the conflict and confrontation. I need to leave the room. I walk to my mom's bedroom at the back of the trailer, holding my young half-sister Mercy. I run my fingers along my mom's belongings. She has so many dusty knick knacks.

    I gaze at her 90s geometric comforter. The thought she will never sleep in the bed again makes my heart sink deep in despair. Mercy squirms in my arms, she is restless, unsure what is happening around her. As I look in Mercy's eyes, I realize, she will never know mom like I will never know my biological father.

Do You know what will happen to my sisters? To their futures?

    I hug her and squeeze my eyes shut. When I open them, I notice my Aunt Barb and Victoria, Mercy's twin, are outside the bedroom window. Barb is waving her hand trying to get my attention, "Hand Mercy to me!"

    "What, why? This is insanity," I shout. "Jerry is going to take them away!"

    I just lost my mom; he can't take the girls too. My emotions spiral, " What am I going to do?" My thoughts are disrupted by a thud in the hallway.

    Roy pins Jerry against the hallway's wood paneling, preventing Jerry from coming after me. Jerry had enough of the tension from my mom's family and decides it's time to leave and he's taking the girls with him. Jerry eventually relents, but during the scuffle someone calls the police.

    The police arrive and a man in plain clothing enters the kitchen and approaches me, my dad, and my Aunt Barb. Detective Scheetz has a full head of black hair, blue eyes, and a plastic white toothpick in his mouth. The toothpick moves constantly from one side to the other. I didn't know it at the time, but Detective Scheetz would be in my life for many years to come.

He is all business. He gets right to the issue.

"What do you want to do with the kids? Put them in foster care or give them to Jerry?"

How can he ask such a question during this chaos? I am only a teenager, 19 years old, only one year into adulthood. My mind flashes back to the conversation with my mom a few months ago. "If anything happens to me, will you take the twins?" I know she wants me to take the girls.

But that's not what Detective Scheetz is asking, it was either foster care or Jerry.

I stare at the wood paneled walls, remembering when my mom first told me about Jerry. They met at a support group for alcoholics. Their relationship didn't last long, but she became pregnant in the two months they dated. She wanted to keep the girls. Eventually, my mom decided Jerry wasn't her type and broke it off.

Detective Scheetz clears his throat. He wants an answer. I nervously hesitate. In my mind's eye, I see a picture. It's my mom jumping up and down screaming, "No! No!" but I don't understand.

I start reasoning in my mind. What would happen to them in foster care? What if they land in a terrible situation with awful foster parents and are abused? I don't want them to be separated. Pam, my mom's cousin, chimes in, "Fathers have rights." The confusion and fear I sense is paralyzing. I am so indecisive. I have conflicting thoughts. I don't want Jerry mad at me, and knowing my mom didn't like Jerry, she wouldn't want Jerry to raise them. I know she wants me to take them,

The Questions

but that's not even an option.

Weeks ago, my mom (and the state of Iowa) made Jerry take a paternity test to confirm paternity. The results confirmed what we all knew and the state would garnish his wages for child support soon. Jerry is the twins' father, but he's a jerk and is unreliable, and my mom needed the child support. He would pop in and out of the girls' lives but at their birth, he demanded the hospital allow him in the labor and delivery room. On all of our birth certificates my mother wrote Roy as the father.

I am so afraid of making the wrong decision. I can't think clearly, yet I have to make a decision. I go against my gut and tell Detective Scheetz, "The twins can go with their father."

Jerry lives twenty minutes away. My half-sisters are only toddlers and he's taking them away from the only home they know. I watch him load his old light-yellow Chevy Malibu with all of my sisters' possessions; their stuffed animals and small matching outfits fall out of the overstuffed garbage bags. I don't know how to feel or think, or even what to say to him. How am I supposed to feel when Jerry wants to take the twins from me?

After Jerry finishes loading his car, we meet on the trailer's rusty steps.

"I will let you see them," he promises. He loads the girls in the backseat surrounded by their stuff, swiftly walks around the car, opens the driver's door, and starts the engine. I am thinking to

myself, "I just lost my mother and now the twins, too." I watch his car slowly pull out of the driveway and turn left off Apache Trail with my two sisters in the backseat.

I stare at the empty driveway. My mom's car will never park here again.

*Are You here with me as tears roll down my face and I feel
abandoned? Did You hear Jerry promise he would let me
see my sisters again?
Are You with me at the accident scene?*

The car accident is a quarter mile from my mom's trailer in the middle of a horse field. Aunt Barb leads us to the scene. I see tire tracks in the green grass where her black Mercury Sable traveled down the steep embankment. I stand at the edge of the road looking down at the field and think there is no way she would drive down such a steep embankment.

Why would she have driven down a steep hill, around a tree, through a white fence and into a big open field? Looking at the tire tracks, it's evident the car maneuvered around the tree. I think to myself how odd this accident is, did she start drinking again? There's no explanation for this. Where was she going? Where was she coming from? Why would she leave Jerry alone with the twins to get him ice cream? Nothing seemed like familiar behavior. How did her car explode in the middle of a horse field? None of this makes sense to me.

I bend down and feel the fire scorched grass. How could this have happened? I'm trying to make sense of this. Then the thought hits me, did she suffer in the fire? Did she pound the glass trying to escape and couldn't? Did she cry for help and no one came? I gaze across the field and then back down at my feet. I see a piece of cracked glass. A smiling black spider and pumpkin decal holds it together. I recognize it's the Halloween window decoration from her car. Shards of glass lay throughout the burnt grass. Fear engulfs me as I imagine her sitting in the car pounding the glass and coughing.

I take it all in, the accident, the tire tracks, the steep embankment, and the car bursting into flames without impact, it doesn't seem like an accident to me.

I get out of my head and it clicks. This wasn't an accident.

Are You whispering in my ear? "It wasn't an accident."

Law enforcement already removed the metal remains of her vehicle and the charred remains of my mother earlier today. Soon results from an autopsy would determine the cause of death. I stand in the black spot where her car exploded, and I feel my own heart explode with every imaginable emotion.

Are You here with me as I crawl into bed, my eyes swollen from crying?

I'm heartbroken and I'm trying to fall asleep for the first time without a mom. I feel utterly alone. I lost my mom, the identity of my father, and my twin sisters all in one day. I'm sleeping with the light on tonight. I'm scared.

Chapter 3

Do You Hear Me?

> *The Lord is close to all whose hearts are crushed by pain, and He is always ready to restore the repentant one. Even when bad things happen to the good and godly ones, the Lord will save them and not let them be defeated by what they face.*
> ~ *Psalm 34:18,19 TPT*

I need Your help, but I don't know if You can hear me. I can't tell if I hear Your voice or if it's my imagination. Help me.

I am lost and heartbroken. I return to the trailer on a mission; to find clues, look for anything amiss that will help me uncover truth.

I look in her bathroom first. I pull the metal plug out of the tub, but I only find her long hair caught in the drain. I hunt for blood stains on the floor tiles, shower curtain, and tub. Nothing. I pull out her black vacuum from the closet, I flip it over to see if anything is caught in the brushes. I sort through the dust and dirt hoping to find anything suspicious. Nothing. Not even a note contemplating suicide. Since she tried in the past, I wonder if this is the final straw. Nothing. I don't initially see anything that created concern. I'm still unsettled but I can't find any evidence why.

Many of her family and friends came in and out of her trailer after she died. Everything is tainted, nothing is in its original position. I continue to search for the unusual, hoping I find something.

Did she record anything on her VHS tapes? My mother loved using the camcorder and recording shows off the television. She transferred songs from the radio to a custom "Sue's Lotsa" cassette tape. She recorded home videos and her favorite TV show, *Unsolved Mysteries* on VHS. She has a mound of VHS tapes. I wonder what her final recording was. Looking through the dates I see one from April 1995, her trip with the girls to the Omaha Zoo. This tape is all I have left of her moving and speaking. Discouragement sweeps over me, I leave her trailer with no new leads.

The Johnson County Sheriff secretary calls, "Hi Sandy, we want your mom's family to visit the Sheriff's office." My fiancé, my stepdad Roy, my brother, and my aunts gather at the Sheriff's office to hear the latest information about my mother's death.

Are You with me in this critical moment of my life?

The medical examiner's report confirms our suspicions. Her death is ruled a homicide! My mother died of blunt force trauma to the head, not by a car fire. The car accident and fire were staged. The fire is a sinister plan to cover up her death. My mother's death is now an active homicide investigation. I utter the only thing I can think of "So, there's a murderer out there?"

I start to panic. How can a murderer walk the streets? The murderer should be behind bars for this heinous crime.

Where is the justice? She was a mother, a daughter, a sister, and she was murdered.

Were You with her when she was murdered?
Do You know who did this? Who would have done this?
How could anyone hate her so much to kill her?

Special Agent Kietzman asks the family easy-to-answer questions. "Did your mom regularly wear a seatbelt?" Everyone chimes in, "Yes she did." I sit looking down at the checkered squares on the linoleum floor. I don't know, we started repairing our relationship before she died. I didn't really pay attention to her seatbelt use.

"When she left the house, what would she take with her?"

Her sister Fern adds, "Her wallet, keys, and for sure her cigarettes."

"Is there anyone who didn't like her?"

Barb brings up George. Mom sued George when he moved her trailer to its current location, tearing up the trailer's metal skirting when he hauled it across town.

My mother won the case a few weeks ago.

Bill continues, "Was she meeting anyone that night?"

Barb interjects, "She planned to meet someone for a bag of pot."

I gasp, "What?! Are you kidding me?!"

I'm mad but I refuse to show it. I thought she stopped using marijuana. I didn't know she still did. How could she do this? She had two little girls to raise. I grew up around drugs; that's the last thing I want for the twins.

The Questions

The detectives interview everyone individually after our group questions. The family separates into different rooms. I follow Bill into a small 10' x 10' room. We sit down and he begins asking me basic questions: about her friends, people she didn't like, new strangers in her life.

"Tell me about the last time you saw your mom," Bill says as he writes on his yellow legal pad.

"The last time I saw her was two days before her death, Saturday, September 23. Wesley and I got engaged and I showed her my ring.

I also mustered the courage to ask her to draw a picture of my biological father before I left her trailer. She agreed she would." Bill jots a few notes down.

I continue, "On September 24, the day of her death, we planned to attend a family reunion, but Wesley didn't want me to go, so I didn't. I felt pathetic, I didn't even call her to tell her I wasn't going. I should have called. I left her hanging. That would have been my last chance to see her alive, and I stood her up."

"Was there anyone she didn't like? Any conflict with anyone?" Bill asked.

I tell him about Jim, "She didn't like him because he molested me as a kid. He was my mom's friend but I don't think he would kill her, it was a long time ago." I take a deep breath, "Oh, and she for sure didn't like Jerry."

Bill is intrigued. "Tell me more." He writes "Jerry" down on the legal pad.

"My mom told me she didn't trust him. A few months ago, she called me, worried he messed with her brakes. I think he was a car mechanic at one time. I know he is a volunteer firefighter too."

"What else did she say about him?" Bill continues to pull

information from me.

"She said he was a peeping tom. One time while he took her to someone's house, she sat in the truck not knowing he looked at a woman through the window. She said he lied often. Jerry said he would be there for her and the girls, but he completely abandoned them. He would steal from the places he worked. My mom was a huge animal lover and Jerry told her he would look for cats to kill. He was just cruel."

While I share all this information about Jerry, Bill is calm and asks neutral questions, almost like he heard this information before. I couldn't tell if my insight made a difference or not.

The detectives question everyone in the family and everyone complies. Then they bring in people outside of the immediate family for questioning. Jerry, Jerry's family and friends, the next-door neighbors, the contractor who moved her trailer. Everyone complies, except for Jerry. He pleads the Fifth Amendment and walks out of the Johnson County Sheriff Office.

Are You with me at her funeral?

Roy helps me with the arrangements. We decide to have her funeral in Iowa City. I've been there before, years ago for my baby sister Erin's funeral. Being next of kin, I'm responsible for the funeral costs. My mother didn't have a will or life insurance. I'm a grieving teenager trying to plan a funeral for my mother. I'm thankful Roy is helping me. The funeral director informs me about the Iowa Victims of Crime Compensation Fund. Since her death was ruled a homicide, the state will pay for some funeral expenses.

I don't want a visitation. There is no body, no casket. Instead we plan a simple funeral for family and friends. I don't want to talk to anyone, but being the people pleaser I am, I stand at the entry greeting everyone before the funeral starts. One of my mother's friend grabs my hand, "I don't know if you know this, but I remember your mother telling me that if anything ever happened to her, she wanted you to have the twins."

"Yes, she told me. But I..." I fumble for words. What would everyone think of me if they knew it was my fault the girls ended up with Jerry? "Thank you for telling me." I say sheepishly and fake a smile.

My mother would be in shock to see so many friends and acquaintances at her funeral. My brother's friends from high school are here, a handful of my friends, most started college a month ago. People love her, in this moment I'm proud to be her daughter.

I feel emotionally drained and we haven't even started the service. The funeral director walks over to my brother and me, telling us it's time to start. My feet are heavy as I walk to the front. I slump to the chair on the left side of the aisle. I feel distant and detached from the situation. I try to convince myself maybe she isn't really dead. I never saw her burned body. Maybe she ran away, maybe this is an elaborate hoax.

These thoughts run through my mind as I stare at my mom's colored pencil self-portrait. I love the violet background, it makes her bright blue eyes pop. I look to my right and I see my mom's biological dad, Alex, and her stepmom Evelyn. My mom didn't have a great relationship with them. Sitting there, I wonder what Alex is thinking.

Does he regret the past like I do?

Looking deeper into my mom's self-portrait I try to think about the good memories. I take comfort in our healing conversation earlier in the year. I saw an Oprah episode on mother/daughter relationships, I apologized to my mom for how I treated her as a growing teen. I was mouthy and she was mean. We fought often and did not share common ground.

When the girls were born, her life turned around for the better and she accepted my apology.

Wesley puts his hand on my knee. It's a comfort to have him next to me. His mom, Rhonda, is here too. They guide me; tell me what to do, tell me when it's time to leave, where we will go next. I can't think for myself and having someone make the decisions for me is a relief.

At the end of the service, we play my mom's Lotsa cassette. Familiar piano chords echo in the funeral parlor, one of my mom's favorite songs, from the famous Liverpool band. The lead singer's gentle voice reverberates in the room. When the lyrics mention "…there's no heaven", I cringe. If there is no heaven—will I ever see her again?

Do You think she went to Heaven?

The Sheriff's Office becomes a regular gathering place for me. I enjoy meeting with Special Agent Kietzman and Detective Mike Scheetz. Their presence is warm and welcoming. They're kind and value what I have to say; it's nice to finally feel valued. I admit I'm obsessed with my mother's case. I want answers. I want justice for her. The thought of someone within my mother's close circle murdering her makes me sick. Who killed her? Why would he or she kill her? Did I send the girls to live with the man who killed her? My questions snowball. They bombard me. I can't eat. I can't sleep.

A search warrant is released for her trailer. My dad, brother, aunts, Wesley, and I wait outside of her home as we watch camera lights flash from the windows. The DCI crime team removes my mother's things one by one from her home. The team is here for a short time and leaves us with more questions. I want to know what they took and why. I see them take journals, photo albums, her black art book, calico carpet pieces, sheets from her bed, they take her side table which sat next to her blue reclining chair.

We enter her trailer after they leave, and I scan the living room. Things are out of place and yet we see something we hadn't noticed before. My Aunt Barb discovers my mom's afghan (made by Grandma) has vanished. It had a colorful zigzag pattern, and mom always slung it over the back of the blue chair, but it wasn't here. Instead, a midnight blue sheet with moons and stars hangs over the chair. My aunt picks up the sheet and we see pieces of the chair are missing. The fabric is cut, and white cushioning is exposed. I never noticed because the sheet covered the new evidence.

I wonder if the afghan is in the laundry area. I open the dryer and find someone else's clothes. I holler down the hallway, "These aren't Mom's or the girls' clothes in here. Whose are these?"

My Aunt Barb runs to the hallway.

"I've been doing my laundry here, it's cheaper," she whispers to me.

I'm appalled. Does she realize I am paying the electric bill?

I'm paying for her clean laundry! I won't say anything because I hate conflict. My aunt is poor. I need to let it go.

There are more important things to worry about.

The afghan is gone. I don't see it anywhere and I start to wonder if my mother died in her home. Was the afghan used to move her body out of the trailer? If that's true, the twins must have slept through it, what a chilling thought.

I head straight to the sheriff's office to talk with Bill and Mike. I'm ready to ask the hard questions now.

"Do you think she died in the blue recliner?" They look at each other, hesitant to share any information.

"If she died in the chair does that mean she saw the person hit her? Did she know she was going to die?" I continue, "Did she see her killer?" I want to know where she was hit in the head.

I know law enforcement won't willingly give me information. Her body told the story of her death and all the lab results weren't back. I know for legal reasons they can't share details of her case. Only the killer—who still walks free—knows what happened that night. I realize I need to manipulate my conversation with the detectives so I can understand what happened to her. I believe if I know the details I will feel better about my loss. Was she caught off guard or did she see it coming? I think if I know exactly what happened to her, I will be at peace and feel better about my loss. Then, maybe I can start to move on.

"Did you need to keep the front of her skull for evidence?"

"Yes, we did." Kietzman says. "We kept all the evidence we needed from the autopsy."

My eyebrows raise, "So she was hit from the front." I get the information that I want but instead of feeling better, I feel torment funneling into my heart. Bill's eyes squint. I know, he knows, I pushed him. I sit down, dizzy by my own discovery.

Goodness, I miss her. I want her back. I want answers to all my questions.

Then there was the last big question I asked her, "Will you draw me a picture of my biological father?"

I imagine how much I look like my father because I don't look like anyone in my family. My mom was a talented artist so I thought she could easily draw him for me.

I need to be alone. I collect my things and walk out of the sheriff's office still in shock and uncertain about the future. How will I continue living with half of my family gone?

I lost four people in one day.

Days pass, questions are unanswered, and I realize it's been one week without her. September fades into October, the cool crisp air reminds me of the season change and the new season without her. October brings an array of beautiful fall colors, first in the tree leaves, then on the ground. I have never lived an October without her.

Halloween comes and goes. No more trick-or-treaters visiting her home being caught off guard by the trick of shaken soda cans. She reveled in the sticky spray secret.

By late fall, our family gathers and goes through her remaining belongings. My dad holds up the angel knick knacks. "Who wants this?" He asks all of us.

"I'll take it, I gave it to her last Christmas."

I accept it begrudgingly.

The angel is wrapped with a ribbon with an inscription 'Love Conquers All'. Her love failed me. She isn't here. I want to blame her for her death, if she hadn't made so many poor choices in life, maybe she wouldn't have died the way she had. I hate having to go through her things, divvying everything up with my family. I don't want to be around family. Why are my aunts here? I want to be left alone with her things. My aunt reaches on top of the refrigerator.

"Your mom made this Christmas gift for you." She pressed the clay onto the tin and created a handmade canister.

"Oh my gosh, this will be the last Christmas present I will ever receive from her," I say. Dread, torment, and truth fill me. Along with the canister, I take a red thermal long sleeve shirt she cross-stitched, a pair of colorful jeans with pennies embroidered, and a few pieces of her art. My brother and my dad take the majority of her art and supplies. Roy has ample storage space at his home. I take the unwanted stuff to the Budget Shop, a secondhand store a few miles down the road.

Her trailer stands empty. Eventually, I turn off the heat. The electricity costs too much and I can't afford the bills. Her trailer feels dark, cold, and lifeless when I walk in. I stand there and think.

Do You know what happened to my mom? Were You with her?

I take a long look at the living room, and then I stare where her blue recliner sat. I wish the walls could talk. I want closure. I close the door and lock it behind me.

I can't sell the trailer for nothing. I place an ad in the newspaper and quickly realize the large number of irresponsible potential buyers in Iowa City. Some forget to show up and don't bother to call. I make endless trips to Iowa City just to be stood up by potential buyers. I end up practically giving it away to a college student for a quarter of the original purchase price.

The house is the last thing I'm responsible for and I tell myself its best to be done with it.

November comes along with the Thanksgiving memories. My first Thanksgiving without my mom reminds me of the last one I shared with her, I insisted on making a turkey.

"I don't eat meat," Her face grimaced.

"I know Mom but it's tradition! I can make green bean casserole, and Banoffe pie."

That year I worked at a tearoom part-time and the 70-year-old owners taught me how to bake and cook (Mom didn't do much growing up and I needed to learn from someone.) So, Wesley, my mom, and the twins had our own little Thanksgiving.

I don't see the girls during the holidays. Just like my mom said, Jerry is a liar. I miss them terribly. I call Jerry and respectfully ask to see my sisters. The day finally comes when I get to see them. Jerry's grandma and sister agree to meet my family at a Four-Wall Church (this is the name I give each church I attend) in downtown Iowa City.

I'm excited. I wonder how they've been. I wonder if he is taking good care of them. My Aunt Barb, Aunt Fern, Wesley, and I meet them. We all sit in orange plastic chairs in the church's nursery. We wait for their grandma to bring them to us. Jerry can't make it. Their grandma carries Victoria, and Mercy is brought in by Melanie. We don't want to overwhelm them, so we initially gaze at them when they come in. Mercy looks at my Aunt Barb, then her eyes move to my Aunt Fern, then Wesley, then me. When her gaze lands on me, her little lip starts to quiver, her eyes fill with tears, and I realize among the familiar faces the only face she wants to see isn't here, our mom's. My heart breaks.

We play with the girls for an hour and then it's time to leave them. They never grant us permission to see the girls again.

The December snow parallels my mother's case; cold with no leads and no new evidence. I wait each day for the phone to ring, hoping an arrest is made. Nothing. I distract myself with Wesley's family for Christmas. I love Christmas with them. The smell of delicious food fills the quaint house before it gets wild and crazy. The candy dishes are full of homemade fudge and pretzels. We open presents in the basement.

Wild chaos erupts when all three kids, two wives, and ten grandchildren unwrap all the presents. Wads of wrapping paper fly through the air. The little grandkids take their bows and stick them on Grandpa K's head, the fun delights of childhood. I'm only 19, celebrating
Christmas without my mom, and I still don't have any answers about her death.

On New Year's Eve, all I can think about is my mother. She wouldn't experience 1996 or any following year. All I want is to return to September 24. I want her back. I want to tell her I love her, I want to share my heart with her. I don't get to hear her share her heart for me. Ever since I was little, we had a tumultuous relationship. There were rough years between us, but she was my mother and I didn't get to say goodbye.

Someone took that moment away from me.

As the ball dropped on TV and we all scream, "Happy New Year!" I think to myself, "How do I go on, how do I move forward from this tragedy? How?"

Do You hear me? I hope so.

Chapter 4

Do You Create Tragedy?

> *I am the Gateway. To enter through me is to experience life, freedom, and satisfaction. A thief has only one thing in mind—he wants to steal, slaughter, and destroy. But I have come to give you everything in abundance, more than you expect—life in its fullness until you overflow!*
> *~ John 10:9, 10 TPT*

Were You there with me when I was a child?
Were You with me every time I heard bad news?

When I look back at my childhood memories, it's difficult to find joy. Tragedy is a constant theme in my life.

Are You the author of all the bad things in my life?

When my baby sister Erin came into the world, it didn't take my parents long to realize something was wrong. I am four years old and Jason is two. She is fussy. Her tears don't stop. My parents try everything: burping, bouncing, putting her in the wind-up swing. Mom and Dad visit several doctors. Finally, the fourth doctor listens to my desperate parents. Erin endures extensive testing, and the doctors discover a congenital heart defect. The doctors determine half of her heart isn't growing. She needs to undergo open heart surgery. The news gets worse. She has a fifty percent chance of survival. The doctors give my parents two options. My dad asks the surgeon which option will be easier on her heart. The surgeon sadly replies that the easiest surgery won't be the most complete. She will need further surgeries if my parents go with the easier one. My dad goes with the surgeon's suggestion for the complete surgery. The surgery is a success, but Erin's heart is too weak to beat on its own and she dies in the operating room.

Mom, Dad, and Grandma Marlene leave the hospital with empty hands, no baby Erin. My mom freezes at the door. She turns around as if to run back and get her. My dad tells his mom to give them some time, so my grandmother returns to their apartment on Emerald Court to be with Jason and me. Time passes and they eventually arrive. Mom pulls Grandma aside, "Did you tell the kids?" Grandma replies with tears in her eyes, "No dear, that is for you to tell your children."

My mom and dad come into our small room in the two-bedroom apartment. My dad tells us," Erin is gone, and we won't see her anymore." Erin never made it to 7 months, a precious baby, gone.

I try comforting my parents, "We will see her again someday." My mother disagrees, "No, we won't." Part of my mother's heart died that day. She was never the same after Erin's death. When I lost my sister, I lost part of my mother, too.

Are You speaking through me when I tell my parents we would see Erin again someday?

Prior to Erin's funeral, our family of four say goodbye

privately. My mom, dad, and my little brother Jason look over her lifeless body. It's wrong to see a little baby so still.

Looking at Erin lay in the little casket hurts my heart even as a four-year-old.

My mother encourages me to touch her.

"It's okay if you want to touch her," my mother gently brushes Erin's hand.

I'm scared and don't want to. I'm afraid death will latch onto me next. Instead, I put one of my favorite toys —a little, stuffed black monkey—in her casket. I don't want Erin to be alone. Even though I'm surrounded by my family, I feel alone and I'm terrified of death.

We donate Erin's crib and baby swing to the hospital. Erin's other possessions are placed in her cedar hope chest. When I feel sad or lonely, I open the chest, inhale the cedar, and gaze at Erin's clothes.

The inscription on her headstone reads,

"A Daughter of Purpose"

I don't understand what the phrase means so I ask Mom to explain it.

Mom bends down to Erin's grave and moves her fingers over the letters.

"Purpose means there is a reason why she was here on earth," she tells me.

"Oh," at four years old I contemplate if I have purpose, too.

I revisit the gravesite under different circumstances after my mom's death. I decide my mother would want to share a headstone with her beloved daughter, so we request to combine them on the marker.

The Questions

    Our lives move on after Erin's tragic death, but our hearts do not. My dad takes a job at a manufacturing plant over in Williamsburg, Iowa, a 25-minute drive from Iowa City. He wants to move the family closer to his job. We rent a turn of the century, character rich, two-story farmhouse. I'm excited about the move. It feels adventurous to live on farmland with tall trees and a creek. I no longer worry about kids from the apartment complex stealing my banana seat bike.

    I love the house on Black Diamond Trail, it's my favorite family home of my childhood. It's crafted with beautiful wood, stained glass windows, push button light switches, and ornate doorknobs. On the outside, it has a creaky front porch overlooking corn fields and wildflowers. It's my real-life dollhouse. The land has a huge old windmill and a working water pump where we retrieve well water. For a long time, I thought my parents called it "whale water". I drink the water but it smells horrible along with the whale visual. Old Man's Creek is down the hill and there is a little forest to the west of the house. Jason and I play in the trees often, on most summer nights until the lightning bugs flicker their lights. The Black Diamond Trail is so dark at night, it's just the brilliant stars above. I'm seven years old gazing at the stars in awe and wonder.

    My favorite part of the property are the two ditches in the front yard, a grassy path separates them. In the summer, wildflowers fill the ditches while big bumble bees fly from one flower to the next. On one particularly picturesque day with the bright sun and a light breeze, I decide to 'hunt' bumblebees. Out of the corner of my eye, I see a rather large yellow and black one. I quickly slide the clear plastic lid over the flower trapping the bumblebee in the butter dish. I hear its frustration. It keeps ramming the lid, trying to escape. I suddenly feel bad for the bee and decide to let it go. I feel cruel trapping a harmless bee. I fling the lid off and run, it becomes free to fly, and it does.

When we're not playing in the yard, we slide down the beautiful foyer banister. If Mom hears our giggles, she knows exactly what Jason and I are doing. Usually we race, seeing who can slide down the banister the fastest. Between the living room and the dining room we discover that hidden pocket doors become useful when the four of us camp in the dining room when the electricity shuts off. Those are the days in the middle of the month when we don't have enough money to pay the bills. My brother and I are clueless though. We love camping with our parents in the house, and the kerosene floor lamp provides all the light we need.

The upstairs bathroom has an old claw-foot tub and a crystal knob on the wooden cabinet. Mom sits us in the tub and fills it with warm water and bubbles.

We splash and twirl, making a mess on the thin carpet bathroom floor. Not much seems to bother her anymore.

Most days she's unusually quiet.

Each room has heavy scrolled metal registers. I remove one from the floor of my room and make a little home for my plastic figurine toys. Inside the floor I create a hidden home for them. Their room has a wooden spool for the table and a washcloth for the carpet. I know when I'm not there, they come alive.

Since Erin died, Dad often brings gifts home for my brother and me. My favorite gift is the Hungry Hippo game. I love trying to chomp the white marbles with my plastic pink hippo. Whoever gets the most marbles in the hippo's belly wins. This kind of joy heals our sadness.

The creek is another healing place for my brother and me.

When it gets unbearably hot in the summer, Mom and Dad take us to play in the cool water. There is always a strange animal encounter at the stream. I find an opossum, not realizing it plays dead. We had a pet squirrel, but one of my dad's band members put a guitar case over the box, suffocating it. We decide to bury it beneath the moss in the little forest west of the house. At the house we have other pets, Jody Dog, another dog named LS, Kat, and a red-eyed rabbit. Unfortunately, the rabbit died by the paws of LS.

A bat swoops down on my brother and me. We scream and run full force down the stairs. My dad swings at the bat with a tennis racquet, knocking it to the ground. We all cheer. Catching, chasing, and accidentally killing wildlife in the farmhouse is a common occurrence.

We all celebrate my dad's tennis racquet hunting skills, and it feels like we're creating the best memories.

Do You see us trying to recover after the loss of Erin?

Growing up on Black Diamond Trail reveals my parents' wild side. They were young when they started our family. Both of them were 19 when I was born. When we moved to the farmhouse, they decided to live out their wild youth. My mom is a bra-less, tree-hugging, hairy-legged animal lover who enjoys sunbathing nude. From a cultural perspective, Iowa is a decade behind, but she catches up to California's standards quickly. She is a dirty blonde enjoying the animals, trees, and the birds and the bees. She is a strict vegetarian and animal lover. Even though the rest of us eat meat, she doesn't like preparing hamburgers, so she asks me to make the patties.

My mother is a waitress at a Little Amana restaurant about ten minutes away. She hates her uniform: a cream top, brown skirt, and apron. She also hates her boss and complains about his wrongdoings.

My dad is a thin good-looking guy. He has a full head of brownish blonde hair and a mustache. Roy enlisted in the Navy, following his dad's footsteps. His dad, Earl, signed Roy up when he was seventeen in San Diego. Roy later resided in Jacksonville, Florida at the Naval base maintaining and fixing helicopters.

Work and play seem to be my father's distraction from grieving Erin's death. My dad spends extensive time at work, eventually climbing the corporate ladder, designing and programming robots. He plays electric and bass guitar in a local band, Foolish Pleasure. Jason and I get to hang out in dark dive bars for sound check—I'm maybe 5 years old—sticky, grungy floors seem exciting at the time. My parents don't think much of bringing us into the bar; maybe they are blinded by their love for the music. I enjoy being out of the house in a new environment despite my introvert tendencies. When I get hungry and want a bag of potato chips, Mom tells me to go ask them. I look down and I can't. I am so shy and unsure of myself, scared to ask anyone for anything.

December 10 becomes the last day I step into the farmhouse on Black Diamond Trail. I will remember this day forever. My parents are at a work Christmas party in Iowa City. Jason and I stay at my parents' friend Lucy's house in Williamsburg. I'm in third grade and Jason is in first. Our parents plan to pick us up after their party, but we never return home. I lay in my babysitter's bed when I hear my mother sobbing, the same deep soul cry I heard when Erin died. I later learn what happened.

My dad received a phone call at the Christmas party, "Your house is on fire!" a neighbor cried. In the small town everyone knew each other and their business. Some of the volunteer firefighters work with my dad at the same manufacturing plant. He quickly tells my mother, and they leave for the 25-minute drive to our house. From Interstate 80, the fire fills the dark sky. Several of my dad's co-workers help extinguish the fire. When my parents arrive, our farmhouse is completely engulfed in flames.

The fire destroys our home. Our only neighbor on the country road, Tom Donahue, thought we were home and broke the front door down trying to save us. The fire is so hot, he doesn't get far before he has to retreat. We lose almost everything. My Cabbage Patch doll and the clothes on my back become my only possessions.

When my parents return to my babysitter's house, they allow us sleep and decide to tell us in the morning. I'm wide awake, hiding in a bedroom, listening to my mother weep. I clench the blanket and cover my ears, trying to protect them from hearing any more bad news.

The next morning my, parents bring us into kitchen and tell us we lost our house in a fire and we will see if anything is salvageable. We jump in our silver Chevette and drive to the Black Diamond Trail.

We pull up to our ravaged farmhouse; our things are still smoldering in the freezing December Iowa air. All of our earthly possessions are piles of ash, resting in the basement. None of us could believe the destruction. One day we have all of our stuff, and the next day nothing is left.

Are You with us as we mourn our beloved home and belongings? Do You see us standing over the ashes stunned, afraid, and heartbroken?

In addition to the loss of our possessions, we lost our two dogs. Jody Dog was a sweet 10-year-old terrier who resembled Toto from the Wizard of Oz. LS was a Great Dane with the nickname "Little Stinker". We also lost our cat, Kat. Jody Dog had been with me my whole life. I don't know what life will look like without him. I ask my mom about how Jody Dog's life ended, "Did Jody Dog burn, did it hurt him?" I could picture him barking at the fire and then running off and hiding under the new sofa we bought a couple of weeks earlier.

"No, the smoke would have gotten to him before the fire," Mom said fast and annoyed.

"Oh." Her words aren't very comforting, and it seems my questions bother her. I picture him lying on the floor barking until the smoke overtook him.

We lost irreplaceable treasures— Erin's handmade wooden hope chest with all of her belongings. A mirror with Erin's little fingerprints (my mother refused to clean it), gone. My brother's favorite baby books, gone. My blue grumpy bear hiding in the register, melted and gone. My Strawberry Shortcake doll and comforter set, gone. My stuffed Garfield doll my grandmother gave me, with the big white eyes, gone. Our baby pictures, birth certificates, any evidence of the life we lived until the fire destroyed everything. We have nothing left.

Weeks later the fire department concludes an electrical fire, originating at our Christmas tree ignited the blaze.

Our house burned two weeks before Christmas Day. Dad and Mom don't have renter's insurance, so there is zero financial compensation for the damages. We are homeless and heartbroken and not looking forward to the holiday. However, something happens that none of us saw coming.

Our community—neighbors on the Black Diamond Trail, friends, friends of friends, my parents' co-workers, kids from my class, even my bus driver, share their kindness, generosity, and love with us. Grandma Marlene, my dad's mom, gathered donations in California and sent us big boxes. My school principal took my brother and me shopping in town and bought us an educational toy. Duke, my bus driver, drove my brother and me to the local Ben Franklin to purchase winter Moon Boots. I cherished them for years. The community gives us everything we need to feel comfortable, but the loss and tragedy still haunts our hearts.

We stay in a hotel for a week, it's all we could afford, and then a local Four-Wall Church invites us to live in their parsonage. We are no longer homeless! The pastor and family move out of the parsonage and across Williamsburg. The Four-Wall Church agrees we can stay in the home until the end of the school year. I didn't know it then, but the Pastor's family would become my second family in high school.

I'll never forget this Christmas. It becomes the most generous Christmas our family ever experiences. We receive a home and an outpouring of kindness and gifts from the community. I lose everything, but it's quickly replaced by strangers.

My parents are speechless. The love from the community is unexpected and wonderful. Barb Schaefer in particular led the community to gather items for us. We feel we owe our small community and especially Barb, so my mother creates art and donates it to the library and local post office to thank Barb and the community for their generosity.

Did You start the fire to teach my family a lesson? Did You send people to introduce us to Your generosity?

In the parsonage, my mother experiences waves of grief. She lost her seven-month-old baby girl and absolutely everything she owned—her memories, her art, her valuables, her identity.

My mother locks herself in her room and rarely leaves. She frequently cries. This stormy season at the parsonage is when lies begin to swirl around my mom. She turns inward and focuses on herself, leaving my brother and me to question our own value and fend for ourselves.

Chapter 5

CAN YOU REDEEM MY LIFE?

Do not fear, for I have redeemed you; I have summoned you by name; You are mine.

~ Isaiah 43:1

My mother started using and abusing drugs and alcohol before I was born. Slowly, she starts spending less and less time with my brother and me. She spirals into her own world, believing the lies. She thinks she has failed as a wife, mother, daughter, and artist. The tragedies are more than she can bear. Alcohol numbs the pain and pot chills her out. I can't bear to be around her when she slurs words and stumbles around the house.

I instinctively know to hide any drug paraphernalia before visitors come to our new house. One Saturday morning, my parents slept in when I heard a knock at the door. I surveyed the room and saw pipes on the living room coffee table and a bag of stash. I hid them under a nearby plastic bowl. I answered the door, and to my surprise it was my dad's boss and wife. They brought us house-warming gifts.

"My parents are still sleeping," I shyly told them.

"Well, give this to them when they wake up." They smiled and left.

Later, when my parents woke up, I told them about the good deed. I wanted their approval.

My childhood involves my own drug use, too. Other people using around me lead to my own experimentation with a mysterious white substance.

In my classroom I see the anti-drug campaigns, "Don't Do Drugs" and "This is Your Brain on Drugs" commercials (remember the egg frying in the skillet?) For the first time, I realize drugs aren't good for my body. I turn down my mom's offer for pot, after a failed persuasion insisting that the queen smokes to relieve pain from menstrual cramps.

At the end of third grade we move to a small town called Ladora, about 25 minutes from Williamsburg. The Marengo school district rivals the Williamsburg School District. I become a River Rat at Iowa Valley Elementary. We move to another farmhouse - this one is on a pig farm so as you can imagine the terrible smell - outside of town. The property has a garden and its fun reaping the benefits. Summer arrives and there is plenty of goodness. Strawberries! Peppers! And Brussels Sprouts! One day I pluck so many strawberries I puke them out of my mouth and nose. I gag at the smell of strawberries for weeks. I love the garden and watching the vegetables grow. I become a farm kid, minus the chores, loving the land and all it has to offer.

My brother catches frogs in the small pond near the

garden. He enjoys watching me scream as he chases me. We play all day outside. It's idyllic. It feels like we are getting close to re-living the days of the country house on Black Diamond Trail.

Did You bring us to this house for redemption? To bring us close as a family after all of the tragedy?

We start feeling more like a family, adjusting to our second country home. Mom creates art and Dad continues his job at Williamsburg Manufacturing. We adjust well at school and make new friends. Life feels close to normal. I am in fifth grade, my brother in third, and one Saturday afternoon my mom asks me to come into their room. I hesitantly walk through their door and notice a letter in my mother's hand. The envelope is beautifully decorated with her hand drawn flowers. I approach them. She hands me the letter. The words inside the envelope are written on simple stationary and are devastating. I read the letter in shock and horror. The letter tells me Roy, the man who is raising me, is not my biological father. It's a horrific revelation and everything I believe to be true about my life feels like a lie. It embarrasses me. I feel shame. I'm confused and I believe the lie that I don't belong in the family and I'm a burden, an unwanted daughter without purpose.

In my mom's handwriting I read, "This is why your skin is darker." My skin color never occurs to me, until now. I look at my tan arms and feel more shame, more humiliation. Roy comes into the bedroom and puts his arm around my shoulders, tells me he loves me, and nothing will change. I don't see it the same way. It already feels like everything is different. I no longer see myself as the same person.

I should have known he wasn't my biological dad. I don't resemble anyone in my family. On special occasions we eat in Amana. An older waitress with short sandy blonde hair and thick circular glasses asks my parents if I'm their daughter. My parents exchange glances and reassure her that yes, of course I am. She awkwardly replies that I don't look like the rest of my family while my parents shrug behind their menus. I just assume she's rude. Now though, I understand why she asks the question. I continue to call Roy "dad" after they share the news, but it now feels forced and awkward. I have questions, but I don't feel comfortable asking either of them. So, I don't.

My mother's substance addiction continues when we move back to Williamsburg and end up in another little country two-bedroom house. We are close to town and the Sundown Lounge, her favorite hangout. She stays out late, drinking and partying, then stumbling home drunk down the long gravel road. Sometimes she is belligerent to my face and screams nonsense at me.

Is this what love looks like? I hate living here and I don't like my life. Can You make it better? Can You bring good from all the heartache?

Despite all the fear at home, I experience a miracle. At 11

years old I travel to California. My parents vacation elsewhere, and I visit my dad's parents, my Grandma Marlene and Grandpa Irvine. On the trip to Newport Beach, a life-changing event happens while I'm with my cousin, Vel. She is ten years older than me, and I adore her. She is beautiful, feminine, and cares about me. I look up to her. She is the total opposite of my hippie mother. Vel is a Southern California beauty queen who introduces me to a world of makeup, perfume, trendy clothes, and most importantly, Jesus.

At the beach she tells my brother and me about Jesus. I've never heard of Him. I don't know who He is. I assume Christmas is about Santa and Easter is about the Easter Bunny. Vel continues to share her experiences as a Christian and I start to feel envious of her life. I want to follow Jesus, too, but don't know how. Vel tells my brother and me that even though we don't know Jesus yet, He already loves us and died for us. Then she asks us if we want to invite Him into our hearts. We both agree and a hunger to know Jesus is born.

The next day I end up with my grandparents at my first professional baseball game. I think to myself, I'm going to test God (I don't recommend this!) I whisper under my breath, "If you are real then let the hitter make it to second base," and he did! I continue these thoughts throughout the game, "Okay if you are real, God, let the home team win." Thankfully, they did!

Vel takes me to her Four-Wall Church and I love it. The congregation is full of surfers singing to Jesus in board shorts and flip flops. I like the casual atmosphere and I am hungry to learn more. I wonder what the churches look like in Williamsburg and if I can meet other Christians like Vel in my small town. I turn to Vel. She is singing a contemporary song with her eyes closed and hands held high in the air. I don't want to leave this Four-Wall Church; I want to stay in the moment forever.

Vacation quickly comes to an end. The thought of returning to Iowa is upsetting. Vel loves and cares for me; she makes me feel special and I don't feel special at home. I bawl like a baby when I board the plane. I feel so alone and hopeless. Traveling home, I read a letter from Vel, she tells me to pray for a Christian friend. I do, and God answers.

My Christian friend turns out to be an entire family. The Lee family is the same pastoral family who offered their parsonage after the Black Diamond Trail house fire. They are a large family (seven kids!) and I love the calmness in their home. They are always kind to each other, loving in actions and words. When the family has a conflict, they talk it out. They never yell like my family does; no slamming doors or screaming fits. The house is in order.

When I return from Southern California, one of the Lee kids invites me to spend the night and attend church the following Sunday morning. It becomes a routine and I frequently stay the night on Saturday and attend church as if I'm their eighth child. At their Four-Wall Church, I decide on my own to take a membership class. I learn the technical side of the religion, the church, the Letters, the Trinity, and baby baptism.

When the subject of baptism comes up in the class, our teacher explains it's a prerequisite to enter Heaven according to this Four-Wall Church. I immediately am concerned about my baby sister Erin. She definitely wasn't baptized, so I ask the teacher.

"She isn't in Heaven because she wasn't baptized, and my parents weren't Christians?"

His response startles me.

"No, she isn't."

My baby sister died and went to hell? Why would I want to love a God who put babies, specifically my baby sister, in hell? Even though I'm confused and disappointed, I continue and become a member of the Four-Wall Church.

Later in my life, through his Letters, God shows me a baby who was never baptized and went to Heaven. When David and Bathsheba's baby died, the Letters don't mention a requirement of baptism. David talks of going to his baby one day. The thief next to Jesus on the cross wasn't baptized either. I spend many years worrying Erin was in hell, but as a teenager after reading these verses, I feel confident Erin is in Heaven.

We move yet again to another house in Williamsburg, this time my parents are proud homeowners. It's the last home we live in together as a family. This classic ranch home has a two-car garage and a cornfield behind the fenced backyard.

This house becomes a house of horrors. My mother ridicules my clothes and my desires to look nice. Clearly, she doesn't agree with Vel. I practically die of humiliation every time she takes me to second-hand stores in Iowa City, mortified at wearing old recycled clothes. At home when I dress up, she frequently reminds me every day isn't a fashion show. I disagree and hope I can get some attention from the boys at school.

In Junior High I become curious about my biological father. My mother occasionally drops hints, but never shares more than a few words. They are random hints, never conveying too much information. One time I dress nice for school and she tells me how I dress like my father. I know what she means but the shame is too much, I don't ask any questions. I realize my father is somewhere far from Iowa. I ask my mom about my ethnicity. She says I'm Filipino. I stare at myself in the mirror and yearn to know the other side of myself.

Do I look like anyone?

At a youth convention in New Orleans, I call my mom and she casually tells me I was conceived in New Orleans. I hang up the phone in shock and look at every man thinking, "Are you my Father?" like the hatchling bird from the P.D. Eastman kids book, Are You My Mother?

When I'm older, Roy tells me the only information he knows about my biological father. A mutual friend named Jimmy Brown owned a trucking company and he connected my mother and biological father. Roy told me they met in New Orleans sometime in September 1975.

In addition to seeking answers about my biological father, I want to learn more about my Heavenly Father. As a teenager and new Christian, I don't have support at home. I don't know how to show love to my mom. Her erratic behavior and drunk tendencies scare me. I become self-righteous at school and home. I look down on people, especially my mother, who drink and party. I believe she has a choice to do bad things and not follow my religious rules. From this religious place in my heart, I judge her and others by my own moral standards.

My mother isolates herself in our basement (she calls it the cave), spending her time painting. She is an incredible self-taught artist, working with many mediums: acrylic, watercolor, clay, and ballpoint pen. I judge her in the art cave, never appreciating her or her art.

My high school years prove to be more tumultuous as my

mother and I grow more and more distant. She spirals deeper into depression and alcoholism, while I lean more on my social status as a popular cheerleader. I value relationships. They keep me outside of the house and are my escape from the chaos and confusion at home. Despite her need to self-medicate, she meets with a counselor at our home.

One specific session, I find a brown bag full of drug paraphernalia. I thought she quit using drugs so I'm angry. I feel betrayed. She lied to me, so I hide the bag outside. My plan is to confront the counselor with evidence she is lying, and prove I can't trust her. I confront my dad about the bag and tell him I hid it. He searches for the stash before the counselor arrives, worried his kids will be sent to foster care.

"My mom is doing drugs, I have proof!" I yell to the counselor as I march outside. I leave the house to retrieve the stash under the tree and its gone. My parents deny the stash and make me look like the liar.

Home isn't a healthy place to live anymore. Things continue to spiral. Mom is arrested for a DUI. We fight all the time. She takes my bedroom door off its hinges so I can't slam it and her cigarette smoke lingers into my room. She calls me "Mouth" and taunts me by singing the Rolling Stones' classic, "You Can't Always Get What You Want". Her message to me is consistent. I should respect her, accept the family I'm born into, and never want more. I am disrespectful. I don't know how to honor her. I'm mouthy and I push her to the edge—maybe over the edge.

One day I notice her wrists bleed as she sits in her blue chair, she's cutting herself with razor blades. She messes with Roy's gun while my brother is home. She takes all her pills, washes them down with liquor, and tries again to end her life. She stumbles down the hallway of a hotel and a good

Samaritan calls the police and saves her life.

My mom is admitted to the mental hospital in Iowa City. I resent her. I hate her. If she wants to die, then she is dead to me. She calls collect from the hospital. I answer only to hang up the phone when I realize it's her. Roy encourages me to visit her, so I go. I'm horrified and never go back. After the mental hospital visit, I ask my dad why he's still with her. He contemplates it and eventually decides to file for divorce. When they release her from the hospital, she moves to a trailer, and I choose to live with my dad.

Despite all my mom's trouble, I don't talk about it at school, I'm afraid to think about what people would say if they knew. I don't want to share my life with too many people. I keep my problems close and only share them with a few of my friends and my boyfriend. I can smile and wear a mask and no one will know. I cheer at wrestling matches, football, and basketball games, all while hiding my inner brokenness. I smile and yell but can only jump two inches off the ground and I become self-conscious cheering at games.

My mask works. No one really knows what my home life is like and I land a spot on Junior Prom Court.

My dad saves the newspaper clipping with my photo, although the caption reminds me that I don't recognize my mother as my parent. It reads, 'Sandy Kersten, the daughter of Roy Kersten is on Junior Prom Court. It's an honor, but I'm embarrassed by my own mother. I don't want to be associated with her. She doesn't support me emotionally, physically, or financially. I can't stand her, and yet I long for a healthy mother/daughter relationship. In high school I need a nurturing mother to lean on, and she is absent. I realize she has nothing to offer me because she is so broken herself. But, I long to be loved, cared for, and to be someone special to my mother.

In my need for someone to mother me, I meet Rhonda. I actually date her son, Wesley. He's a year younger than me, good looking, and charming. I'm obsessed with our relationship. Wesley and I are inseparable. He has the most wonderful family. His mother is so attentive to her children. She cooks and cleans for them, helps them with their homework, and is involved with their youth group and Sunday school. As a family, they play board games together. In the winter they ice skate on the frozen family pond. They show up for school performances and science fairs. I have no idea families interact with so much joy or support for each other. Rhonda treats me as one of her own; I'm a daughter to her. She gives me a place to escape from the chaos of my own family.

My senior year is an exciting time. I'm the first on my mom's side to graduate from high school. Mom and her sisters all dropped out of school at a young age. I'm especially proud to be the first woman to graduate.

At the beginning of my senior year, I'm voted onto Homecoming Court and ride in a red convertible for the parade. I buy a velvet dress, curl my hair, and smile and wave to the crowd, looking for familiar faces. I wear a confident mask well, but inside I'm insecure and afraid, feeling undeserving of the nomination to Homecoming Court.

At the end of my senior year, I'm voted Prom Queen. My class picks me, Sandy Kersten. Similar to Homecoming, excitement fills me, but again I feel like a fake imposter. If my own family doesn't value me or see my worth, then do I deserve this title? Sandy, the Prom Queen, doesn't fit with my own insecurities. I feel unworthy of Prom Royalty and my sparkling crown.

Did You see me as royalty? Are you trying to show me how You see me?

Despite my insecurity, I attend prom five years in a row, the fifth year returning as a graduate and passing the crown to the next Queen.

Graduation is a positive memory with my mom. She attends and hollers my name in front of everyone when I walk across the stage and receive my diploma. I can feel her pride and I want her to be there. Things quickly shift when she becomes pregnant and sober. For my graduation gift, she gives me a gold rose ring with a small diamond in the center. It's her ring, and as a kid I asked her if I could have it when she died. At my graduation it's apparent she is having twins. After my parents' divorce, my mom met Jerry. They dated for two months and she became pregnant, starting a new life in Iowa City.

The summer of 1995 I want to attend college. I apply and receive scholarships but I have a horrible fight with my dad and move out early. Even though I work three jobs, money is tight. I have first and last month's rent and a deposit for electricity. I use my scholarship money for my new place. Michelle, my good friend, and I become roommates. I delay college and reject an offer from Michelle's parents to pay for my tuition. I don't want to owe anybody anything and I'm afraid I'll
disappoint anyone who invests in me.

That summer on an airplane, I meet an executive opening a Brooks Brothers outlet store in my hometown. He gives me his card and tells me to reach out for a job. When I return from my trip, I apply and start a part-time position. Eventually I land a full-time job and become a key holder. I open and close the store and the position is a big deal for me. I don't have self-confidence, but Rhonda encourages me to take the job. She truly believes in me.

Living on my own and employed, my relationship with my mother continues to mend. We attend a makeup event, just the two of us, while her friend watches the twins. We have a great time putting on different shades of lipliner and eyeshadow. I want her to have the entire skin care system I use, so I buy one for her with the little spending money I save. After the event, as I drive her home, she looks over at me.

"You should become a beauty consultant, Sandy. You would be so good at it!"

Flattered, I think about it for a second, it would be kind of fun, but I remind myself that I don't have the confidence to do it. Plus, Wesley wouldn't really call it job security.

As we continue driving, I decide to address my disrespect from my younger teen years. I saw an Oprah show about mothers and daughters reconciling and I decide I would apologize.

"Mom, I'm sorry for my attitude and disrespect when I was growing up."

She listens, but never offers a counter apology for all of her wrongdoings. I personally feel a weight lift and I want a close relationship with her. I drop her home and we don't really say much else about it.

Wesley and I are still dating. Our relationship isn't healthy, there are no boundaries and I have my own baggage and grief to sort through: loss, betrayal, my parents' unhealthy relationship, and my personal insecurities. I want to escape the chaos in my life and I want someone to tell me what to do, so I lean on him.

I also want someone to take care of me. Wesley has a strong

personality and I let him control my life. After he graduates (early) from high school and signs up for the Army Reserve, Wesley starts talking about marriage. I feel torn, relieved not to be single, but hesitant to dive into a marriage with a controlling partner. An older friend recommends I talk to a youth pastor about marrying Wesley. The youth pastor suggests I share my concern with him and request we revisit the engagement idea in six months.

"I'm only going to ask you once," he replies in anger. I wish I had waved goodbye, but I do the opposite. I love his mom and family and try to convince myself it might be fine.

So, when he turns 18, he does exactly what he said he would do. He asks me to marry him right in the stock room of the outlet store. Two weeks after the engagement, I visit my mom in Iowa City to show her my ring and visit the girls. Mom is excited about our engagement and she gives us a card, "Congrats on your future marriage! Now when are you going to have kids?" We laugh and hug and I feel so blessed to share the moment with her.

While I'm with my mom, I'm thinking about the one other thing to mention before the night is over. I'm inspired by a conversation with my boss, Patty from work. She suggests my mom draw pictures of her grandkids.

"I know you want to find your biological father, you should ask your mom to draw a picture of him!"

I think it's a brilliant idea. My mother is talented, and this would be easy for her. My mom didn't have any photos of my biological father nor had she given me a name, but maybe she could remember what he looks like and draw him.

That day in her trailer, I drum up the courage before we leave.

"Can you draw a picture of my biological father?" I ask

nervously.

She pauses for a moment. I'm worried she will reject the idea. I want to see who I resemble. I have dark skin, hair, and brown eyes instead of her blue eyes and blonde hair. She looks hard at me and agrees. I'm beyond excited, what a wonderful gift this will be!

We make plans to attend a family reunion the following day. I tell her I'll see her later and we part ways.

This is the last time I see my mother. Wesley doesn't want me going to the family reunion because we have other business to attend. I forget to call my mom to tell her I won't be there.

The following morning, I receive the 4:00 am phone call from my dad.

What will You do with this mess of a life I have? Can You show me value in any of it?

Chapter 6

CAN YOU HEAL MY HEART?

He heals the brokenhearted and binds up their wounds [curing their pains and their sorrows].

~ Psalm 147:3 Amplified

I'm searching for comfort from my past. I need to know someone cares about all I've been through. I am missing something. Pieces of my heart seem flung all over. I don't know how to create a good life. I went against my better judgment and married Wesley three years ago. This relationship isn't right. The marriage isn't going well. I know I'm not a supportive wife, but I also don't feel supported. I'm fragile and concerned my own needs aren't met. Wesley and I get into horrific fights; the house ends up destroyed. He controls my spending, I don't know what I can or can't buy. I'm 23 years old and he reprimands me for buying books.

After my mom died, I decide to pursue my passion for esthetics. I see a commercial on TV for a spa in Cedar Rapids.

Spontaneously, I make an appointment and as I'm receiving the facial, I tell the esthetician I want her job. She puts me in touch with the manager and I learn that a small scholarship is available if I graduate from esthetics school and work at that spa. So right then and there I decide to go back to school. I move in with my grandparents in Arizona to start esthetics school. I want to attend a local beauty school, but esthetics are new to Iowa and there isn't a developed school in the area. I want to take control of my career, so I temporarily move to Arizona. Wesley protests and throws fits on the phone about our distance, but I stick it out, graduate, and work at the spa. I love my work. I find purpose in making others feel good about themselves, and it's a welcome distraction from life outside the spa room.

    I often look at our marriage under a microscope trying to see the good things. For instance, I still love his mom, Rhonda. Since high school she has treated me like a daughter; buying me gifts for Christmas and Valentine's Day, and on my birthday we go out to eat. She's always thoughtful and gentle, never mean and distant. Another positive in our relationship is spending the holidays with Wesley's family. Wesley's grandparents, aunts, uncles, and fifteen cousins gather on Christmas Eve. It's a full, fun house. Grandma K makes candies and homemade fudge, and the house smells divine. I never experienced that as a kid. My favorite moment happens after all presents have been unwrapped and a wrapping paper war ensues. Balled up wrapping paper bounces off Grandpa K's head. The family hollers and razzes each other but there is so much love between them. Growing up, my family opened presents at home and the family gathering died when my mom's parents died. My dad's side lived so far away we didn't share holidays together. Wesley's family cares about each other. I desire comfort and connection and his extended family offers it. I know this is one of the main reasons I married him, for his family.

Wesley and I move to Oklahoma. He's been transferred for work as a salesman for his father's fitness company. I feel so alone and it's the first time in my life I'm afraid of being alone. I don't know anyone here in Oklahoma. I cry every day. The house is small, a 1950s-style two bedroom on William Drive. I often call my mother-in-law. Her voice is a comfort when I feel lonely. One day, I answer the door and there she is. Rhonda surprised us, and I felt beyond grateful to see a familiar face.

Immediately upon arriving in Oklahoma, I approach a local day spa to offer my facial services. The owner, Dessie, offers toning tables, tanning, and body wraps. The thought of adding professional services is good for business. I pay $125/month for rent and charge $35 for facials. Initially, I'm scared to be a business owner. I take out a loan with my brother-in-law, purchase a spa steamer, table, skin care products, and a wax pot, among other supplies. I have zero confidence in myself. I've never been a business owner before, but I love giving facials.

When Rhonda arrives, we enjoy decorating my new business, creating the space, decorating with comfy linens, candles, a stereo projecting the sound of the ocean. It's my space, my business. I look around and think to myself, wondering if I can turn things around; if good things will start to happen and my heart will heal itself. I wonder if I can have a good life doing something I love.

Dessie often comments on my marriage. "Wesley will never change. He's controlling. I wouldn't put up with that!" At work she mutters, "A leopard doesn't change his spots. He will always control your money and your time if you let him. This is not how things are supposed to be."

I usually shrug my shoulders, not sure how to respond.

My co-workers and I plan a girl's weekend trip to Dallas, lots of shopping, and a salon visit, but Wesley throws a fit. He doesn't want me leaving and he doesn't want me spending money, and ironically, he's out of town himself. I can't do this anymore and it's the first time I think I'm really over this relationship.

After our fight about the trip, I decide to leave him. I color my hair blonde, a bold look for my bold decision. The process takes forever, and the end result is awful, blondish orangish completely damaged hair. Wesley takes one look at me and dismissively asks how much my bold project cost. I know he'll be upset. He turns around and walks away, leaving me feeling abandoned and rejected. He never accepts me for who I am, and my physical appearance always matters to him. My hair color experiment affirms my decision to leave.

Today is our four-year wedding anniversary. Wesley is out of town and I'm packing up my things, preparing to leave him.

I'm tired of living like this. Will You forgive me for this decision? My heart hurts from all the turmoil, I can't take anymore.

While moving my stuff out of the house, I see the red light flashing on the answering machine. There are fifteen messages on the machine, he must know something is up. He continues to call, I stare at the phone, contemplating picking it up. Instead of answering, I decide to listen to a few messages while I pack up, the last message stops me in my tracks.

"I am on the ledge of a building and I will jump."

I drop everything and drive to my friend's house. Diane and TJ answer the door, my eyes are red, and tears stream down my face. I barely communicate the words to them.

"He's going to kill himself. He left a message on my machine. We need to call the police in Las Vegas," I cry.

Diane and TJ know this is Wesley trying to manipulate the situation. I don't understand. I call my neighbors, Jace and Lydia, Jace is a police officer and Lydia is studying to be a lawyer. They meet me at Diane and TJ's home, everyone is reassuring me that Wesley won't attempt suicide. They all agree he's just saying it to hurt me.

"He wouldn't't just say that! He knows how much it hurt me when my mom attempted suicide," I cry.

My mind flashes back to my mom's suicide attempts and I realize my friends are right, Wesley is manipulating the situation. He has no intention of killing himself. The threat is too close to the agony and chaos my mom created in my adolescence. I realize, this isn't what love looks like. So today, on my four-year wedding anniversary, I file for divorce and leave Wesley. As I'm pulling out of the driveway, I whisper under my breath, "I'm free."

Chapter 7

Can I Have My Own Family?

*To the fatherless, He is a father.
To the widow, He is a Champion-Friend!
To the lonely, He gives a family…*
~ Psalm 68:5,6 TPT

Wesley initially resists the divorce. He calls everyone, my dad, my stepmom, my grandma and grandpa, and my friends asking them to convince me to change my mind. He finally relents and signs the papers and we officially are divorced in a few weeks. The one thing I will never regret about my marriage to Wesley is it led me to Oklahoma. Even though saying goodbye to Iowa and familiarity was painful, I've met dear people who changed my life.

After the divorce is finalized, I decide I want to have some fun. I get involved at the Four-Wall Church. I know church might not be a college-aged woman's first choice for fun, but I've made a new group of friends and I'm happy. Occasionally, I contemplate moving back to Iowa, but after a conversation with a friend I realize I'm blessed living in Southwest Oklahoma. I'm doing well as a self-employed esthetician. I've met some great people at the Four-Wall Church. For the first time ever, I enjoy going to church.

The music is less somber than the staunch traditional Four-Wall Church I attended in Iowa. People smile while they sing, they even stand up and clap their hands. I love the song "God is Good, All the Time." I enjoy clapping, singing, and checking out the church goers' outfits— all of them dressed up. I see many of my clients from the day spa at church. My motives are wonky but it's a good place for networking.

As a twenty-something, I feel free to be silly and find myself. I celebrate turning 24, and my roommate Ericka and her sister Jen throw me a Hook themed birthday party. They blindfold me and lead me down to the creek and the next thing I know mashed potatoes cover my face. They re-create the movie scene when the Lost Boys sit down to have dinner and a food fight ensues with Robin Williams. My friends set up different food stations— spaghetti, mashed potatoes (my new boyfriend, Josh spearheaded the mashed potato station), birthday cake, and whipped cream, and it's a beautiful mess. We all jump in the creek to clean up. It's the best birthday to date.

I first met Josh at a church event. I was the tour guide for a dramatic play at my Four-Wall Church's version of Halloween. As the tour guide, I would lead attendees to different hypothetical scenes before and after they died. I remember Josh leaning up against the wall with his hands nervously behind him as we waited to move to the next dramatic scene.

"Hi, I'm Josh. I've seen you around church."

Later I would learn he had witnessed my baptism a few weeks earlier. I wanted to rededicate my life to God after getting a divorce, I felt I had sinned and wanted a fresh start. Josh told his buddy Quentin, "I'm going to marry that girl."

I hadn't noticed him.

"Oh really? I'm Sandy. I moved here about a year ago from Iowa," I reply coolly.

"From Iowa? You don't look like military, what brought you here from Iowa?"

Altus is a military town and it's assumed most newcomers are affiliated with the military. I don't want to explain the whole story or my divorce, so I continue playing it cool.

"I moved down with a friend and I started my own business as an esthetician at the day spa."

"That's cool."

"What do you do?" I shoot back.

"My dad and I own a flying school and small airplane service called Altus Aircraft. You should come flying with us sometime," he offers.

"Yeah, sounds fun." I smile, looking forward to the date.

Our first date is on a small Piper plane a few weeks before Christmas. We fly across the Oklahoma plains as festive holiday lights twinkle below us. It is four months after my divorce. I am feeling so excited on our first date, it is so adventurous and very out of my comfort zone as far as first dates go.

Josh is a mechanic at his dad's business. His warm smile and pretty blue eyes give any uneasy passenger a sense of calm. I've never met anyone who makes me laugh like he does. I've been through so much in the last few months, and his jokes and lighthearted personality take away the pain in my heart.

Our chemistry is magnetic, yet we're so opposite. I feel tiny standing next to him. He's a whole foot taller than me. Besides our height difference, he's fair skinned, and I have a dark complexion. I'm a morning person, he's a night owl. I'm a regular church attender and he sporadically goes. I follow the rules (even the unwritten ones) and he's a rule breaker. We've been together for three months and I like Josh, although he knows I'm not ready for a commitment.

I feel damaged and uneasy about my past, and also wondering who would want to be with someone who's been divorced. I have concerns too, about his interest in our relationship.

Sometimes he feels close and engaged, other times he pulls away and I feel like I'm the problem, like I need to try harder or I need to say the right thing. Sometimes I don't understand him, and it makes me unsure of myself. My insecurities get the best of me and I call off the relationship.

A few weeks later a threatening Oklahoma storm approaches our hometown when I receive a text from Josh.

"How are you doing with the storm? I know you don't like them."

"I'm alright."

"Do you want to come over?"

I start to text something else, then change my mind.

"Sure, I'll be over."

I miss Josh, I think I still have feelings for him. I'm excited to see him again. I'm willing to push aside our differences and try to move forward. We talk on the couch, meaningless small talk, then he leans over and kisses me, "I miss you."

It's all I need to hear. The butterflies and tingles race through my body.

"I miss you, too," I whisper back.

Just like that, we're back together again.

It's Sept. 19, 2001, six months after the Oklahoma storm. Josh sets up a family outing on the plane. His dad pilots the Piper, a six-seat plane, and flies all of us to Lawton, Oklahoma. I'm joined by his stepmom and two sisters. We land in the little airport, collect the rental car, and drive to their family's favorite restaurant for a celebratory meal. Nikki, Josh's younger sister, is in town. Her husband is deployed overseas so the family wants to gather and keep her company. It's not my favorite restaurant. I hate seafood but everyone wants to go, so I bite my tongue and figure I'll order a salad. We start the meal with a prayer and enjoy each other's company over dinner.

After dinner, we drive back to the airport and begin the short flight home. The night sky is gorgeous; it's jet black and stars fill the sky. As we begin the descent, Josh tells me to look out my window. I see with my own eyes, right there, on top of the airplane hangar written in Christmas lights are the words, "Marry Me".

Oh, my goodness! I'm thrilled!! We get out of the plane and Josh gets down on one knee.

"Will you marry me, Sandy?" he asks.

"Yes! Of course, yes!" I shout with excitement.

Beaming, we leave the airport and drive to college group night at our church. Nikki joins us and during the altar call,

Nikki professes her faith and accepts Jesus as her Savior. What a night this was turning out to be! After the service we share our good news with all of our friends. I show off my platinum oval, cathedral-style mounted diamond. Six smaller diamonds surround it. It's the most beautiful ring I've ever seen. Throughout the service I catch myself obsessively staring at it.

We didn't want to wait long for the wedding, so we set the date three months later, December 1, 2001.

Our wedding day shares the high school football state championship. The Altus Bulldogs are in the tournament and only 20 percent of our guest list is here, I guess there's a lot of local football fans. It's a little disappointing, I've spent so much of my own money on this wedding and I lose my guests to high school football.

Dessie (the owner of the spa) is my maid of honor. As we're getting ready, she whispers in my ear, "If you want to run away, I will take you away."

"Oh no! I love Josh, I want to be his wife," I reassure her. "I don't have that I'm -going-to-regret-this-for-the-rest-of-my-life thought like when I married Wesley."

Shannon (also from the spa) is my personal attendant. Shanda, a spa client, is my friend and wedding photographer. My old roommate Ericka is here with her new husband. My family is here: Roy, my stepmom Monica, my Aunt Fern, my Aunt Barb and Uncle Tony and their kids. Josh's high school friends are here and his extended family, too. It's small but it doesn't matter, the Four-Wall Church looks beautiful since it's decorated for Christmas. We exchange vows, and when Josh says his, I can see in his eyes he means every word. I slip his ring on his finger. It's engraved with Col. 1:17. Our loved ones circle around us and pray.

I feel Your Presence, are You with us?

The Four-Wall Church doesn't allow dancing at the reception, so we have wedding cake with our small group of friends and family. So many tables are empty, it's disappointing, but I look at Josh and realize I married a man I truly love.

As we leave the church, Josh tells me he needs to give his mom a ride home. My face turns blank, I'm speechless.

Instead of a formal send off to the getaway car, Josh drives his mom home. I drive myself home in my wedding dress, my heels pressing the gas, wondering why my new husband left me alone. He didn't choose me.

I pull up to my apartment, and my Aunt Fern is packing up her things.

"What are you doing here?" she asks, confused to see me.

I act like everything is fine.

"Oh Josh ran his mother home and I'm going to meet him at his house."

I quickly change the subject.

"Thank you so much for coming down to Oklahoma for my wedding, it means so much."

"Well, of course, you are my favorite niece."

I know the main reason my mom's side of the family made the 12-hour drive is because they feel bad that my mom isn't here to celebrate my wedding day.

"I wish mom could have been here. Do you talk to Detective Scheetz much?" I ask, curious if she stays in touch.

"Occasionally I call him, he says there is nothing new about the case." Fern's face seems without emotion. It has become the new normal, now six years since her murder and law enforcement still hasn't made an arrest. Living far away from the situation makes it easier to ignore. I'm not reminded daily of my mother's death. Aunt Fern gathers her clothes and lifeline of tea. I hug her goodbye and now I'm alone in my apartment.

My insecurity seeps out as I gaze at my thin body in the mirror. I whittled my way down to 106 pounds for the wedding. I took diet pills daily and ate only when necessary to keep myself from fainting. I know Josh wants me to look good and I assume he will stay with me for the long haul if I'm attractive and thin.

I look back at the mirror and snap out of it, gather my makeup and luggage in the apartment and head to Josh's house. He isn't ready when I arrive. As he packs for our trip, I talk with his mom. She assures me she'll go back to the church and clean up. I'm so thankful I don't have to worry about it. We say our goodbyes and drive away in my avocado green Saturn. Our honeymoon destination is Dallas. Once we're out of Altus, on the highway, we relax and I'm elated to be married to the man I love!

Will You bring Your goodness into our marriage?

We're married nine months when I learn I'm pregnant, expecting a baby boy in July. I enjoy being pregnant. Feeling the little kicks and watching a wave move across my belly. Everyone says I'm beautiful and glowing. In those moments I long for my mom. I have so many questions for her. Did I come early? Was she nervous about labor and delivery? Was it painful? I quickly remember my baby won't have biological grandparents.

One June morning at 8:00am I wake up and head to the bathroom, my underwear is damp. Oh goodness, I wonder if my water broke, but it's too soon I have five weeks left of my pregnancy. I immediately think of my friend Shannon, she was sent by helicopter last week to Oklahoma City, she was six weeks early.

Frantic, I wake Josh, I beg him to get out of bed and take me to the hospital. He's too tired.

"Call me and let me know if it's time."

I can't wait a moment longer, so I waddle out to the car and drive myself to the hospital. I haven't even packed an overnight bag, this is happening too soon. What if the baby and I will be flown to Oklahoma City, too? Fear takes over my thoughts. This isn't supposed to be happening. Will the baby be okay? So many questions haunt me as I drive myself to the hospital.

I check myself in at the hospital and the nurse puts me in a wheelchair.

"I'm hoping this is a false alarm. I'll call my husband, if it turns into a big deal," I say matter-of-factly.

She wheels me to the maternity ward. The nurses help me

move over to the bed. The nurse does a pH test strip to see if indeed my water broke. It's leaking. I realize at this moment I'm going to have a baby soon. I hate being alone. I think as I stare at the tiled ceiling.

Your Letters say, I'm not alone but this is such a big moment and I could use some support.

Why is the baby coming so early? Fear is guiding me. My thoughts race to the night we celebrated my 27th birthday, maybe it was soaking in the hot tub. Or possibly, the bumpy drive on the mud-filled country road caused it from the night before?

Josh arrives at the hospital. I'm hooked up to a monitor to record my contractions. The birth starts escalating. Its 10:00am and I remember I am the leader of an 11:00am Bible Study. I call Shanda.

"I'm in labor so I won't be teaching this morning. Please have all the ladies pray."

I hang up the phone and I'm hit with another strong contraction. Suddenly, it's time to push. I'm scared.

"Somebody help me," I scream. I transition so quickly. I only push three times and at 11:18am baby Joshua arrives, making his debut five weeks early. He is a healthy baby boy and weighs 5 lbs.11oz. He is perfect. The nurse places him on my chest and I have a moment to stare. My biggest hope and fear rolled into one word, mom. I have my family.

Later, when the nurse brings baby Joshua to me, she shares how Josh could be a poster husband for helping a wife through labor. His intuition and helpfulness were commendable. With baby Joshua in my arms I sing "Happy Birthday" to my sweet baby boy and then "Father, I Adore You." While I was pregnant with Joshua, I created a Praying God's Word Booklet. I gathered scriptures to pray over him.

The long hours at the hospital are taking a toll, but I'm determined to breastfeed Joshua despite his preemie struggles. Because he is five weeks early, he didn't fully develop the breastfeeding reflex, so I tape a tube to my pinky and push my breast milk through a syringe into his mouth. As soon as it becomes familiar, I nurse him.

When we bring baby Joshua home from the hospital, I am nervous (probably like every other new mom) as thoughts of my own mother's staged car accident quickly enter my mind. Fear seems to follow me. Josh drives us home and I stare at his itty-bitty body in the blue car seat carrier. We make it to the driveway, and take him inside to his new home.

Months before Joshua was born, Josh enlisted in the Oklahoma Air Guard and committed two weeks a year for active duty and one weekend drill a month. He leaves on Friday and returns the following Sunday night. I'm not emotionally or physically ready for Josh's guard drill weekend to start the same day we bring our baby home from the hospital.

"Please stay!" I beg.

He insists he needs to go. I don't know what to do with a brand-new baby.

"God, please help me," I pray.

I'm exhausted from lack of sleep and I don't know how to care for Joshua. What if he starts crying and won't stop? I don't have anyone to lean on. No husband. No mom. No mother-in-law. No one. I drift off to sleep and startle myself awake. My eyes meet Joshua's big brown eyes staring at me. I smile. I want a man to love me forever and I have created one. My forever family.

I take each hour as it comes. Joshua and I make it through the first night. However, the next day is the fourth without substantial sleep. I start hearing voices. My hormones are wacky after giving birth.

I call Josh.

"Please come home. I can't take it, I'm hearing voices, I need to sleep."

He agrees and comes home hours later. Josh watches Joshua while I sleep. When I wake up, I'm in love. Josh is sleeping with Joshua laying on his chest. I always knew Josh would be a great dad. The sound of my feet on the tile wakes Josh.

"How are you doing? Feeling better after some sleep?"

"I'm much better with rest and seeing my two boys."

Joshua's arm is free from the blanket. I watch as Josh is particular about how he tightly swaddles Joshua. He looks like a little peanut. Joshua is my peanut. It makes my heart melt. We're a family. I finally have my own family.

Our family continues to grow. Josh and I have two more children, Karis Evelyn born in 2005 and Kingston Justus born in 2007. I immediately fall in love with each one. I pray for their future spouses, fulfilled lives, and I pray they don't endure the pain I've suffered. I pray they won't need a heart healing. I want them to have a better life than I have had. I pray angels watch over each of them, and they fulfill each of their destinies. My heart holds my family close and I pray they become people of character and integrity who serve Him.

Josh comes into the kitchen and watches the kids. I collect the plates from breakfast and get the trash from under the sink.

"I'll be right back, going to take the trash out."

As I walk to the dumpster, I recognize our next-door neighbor, Marian Evelyn. She's also taking her trash out. I realize she's much older, probably in her eighties, and her beauty radiates as she smiles at me and starts up a conversation about our dog.

"Honey, you sure have a big dog. What is his name?"

"Solomon."

"Like King Solomon in the Bible?" she asks.

"Yes, we wanted a strong name."

"Well, Praise the Lord, honey."

I never met anyone who said that. She is obviously a Christian, I think to myself.

"Can I come over to your house?" The words jump out of me.

"Well, sure honey, you are welcome anytime."

I feel a sense of urgency, "Alright, how about tomorrow afternoon?"

"Sure honey, that'll be nice. I'll have some ginger ale ready for you."

My emptiness aches for the welcoming kindness she exudes. Is she my neighbor for a purpose? At the dumpster I make a new friend and I start counting down the hours until I can see her again.

Part Two

The Facets

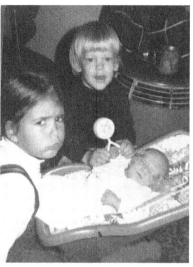

Sue & Sandra
1977

Sandra, Jason and Baby Erin
1981

Williamsburg Journal Tribune 1984 Caption reads: A TOTAL LOSS - A young rural Parnell family, The Roy Kerstens, lost all their belongings in a fire that destroyed their home one mile west of Holbrook on the Black Diamond Trail, Monday night, Dec 10. Four family pets - two dogs and two cats - also died in the fire, still smouldering Tuesday afternoon when viewed by the Kersten family. Shown above are Roy and Sue Kersten, both 27, Sandy, 8 and Jason 6.

The Kersten Family
Roy, Sue, Sandra & Jason
1983

Roy & Sandra
1986

Marian & Karis
2005

The Rohrer Family - Josh, Sandra, Joshua, Karis & Kingston
2008

Sandra searching for her biological father with
the help of supporters on Facebook
2019

Chapter 8

TEAR COLLECTOR

You've kept track of all my wanderings and my weeping, You've stored my many tears in Your bottle, not one will be lost. You care about me every time I've cried. For it is recorded in Your book of remembrance.
~Psalm 56:8 TPT

Have You brought Marian and I together?

I take meandering steps back to my house as I mull this over in my mind. Reflecting on the afternoon and the conversation we share, I'm in shock. I walk up to my porch and see a beautiful pink vase at my doorstep. I need to sit down and replay the afternoon's events in my mind.

I walk over to Marian's white brick, 1950s ranch home. My hand is slightly shaking as I knock on the door. I notice a metal fish nailed to it the words, "May the God of Peace dwell in all who enter here." I think to myself, "I need peace in my life."

Marian answers the door in her polyester pants and a knit sweater with a little rose brooch. She directs me to her davenport, a cream, pink, and blue patterned L-shaped sofa snuggled into the large rectangular room. Light beams in from the generous picture window. True to her word, she offers me ginger ale and a seat on the sofa. Her southern hospitality wins me over, she acts as if we are long-time friends. I love her kindness. She is so full of peace!

Are You peaceful like this?

I set foot in her living room and my nerves suddenly rest. Marian has no frilly decor, just subtle and sparse antiques. Everything is still and quiet, it's a new sensation to me. I've never experienced tranquility in a home like this before. I don't recall experiencing peace in my life either. I immediately feel at home. Although she is still a stranger to me, I feel comfortable around her. Sitting on her sofa, I sense I'm in a safe place a refuge from life.

An art piece catches my eye, propped up on the brick fireplace.

"Did you just get that?" I ask.

"Yes, I mentor a man and he thought this was a good verse for me."

I read it out loud.

> *"Tremendous power is released through the passionate, heartfelt prayer of a godly believer."*
> ~ *James 5:16*

"Those are powerful words," I add.

Marian leans into me and says matter of factly, "Honey, I don't pray for anything I don't think will happen. As sure as I'm talking to you, He hears me, and His love and caring heart are real."

It's at this moment she tells me about the Tear Collector.

Marian gushes, "The Tear Collector is loving and kind. He collects each of your tears, dear. He cares for you."

She continues for hours on the stories of His love, but it's not only her words sparking life in me, it's her actions. She listens without making judgmental comments. I share the feelings I carry after the divorce and remarrying.

I share my struggles as a new mom.

"What if my kids hate me, like I hate my mom?"

With truth in her eyes, Marian reminds me that I'm not my mom. She tells me I will parent differently. Her words resonate in my heart. It's true, I'm not my mom. Things will be different with my children.

Are You disappointed in me for divorcing and remarrying?
Have I cursed myself?

I tell Marian the judgement I feel at the Four-Wall Church. I tell her people stare at the new life I started. Marian accepts me for who I am. She doesn't seem to care that I have remarried, she loves me exactly where I'm at. I don't feel ridiculous when I ask questions. I can feel her unconditional love and it's unusual to me to hear about the Tear Collector's love.

"Honey, love never fails. Never!" Her authority infuses the phrase, and I truly believe what she says.

Tear Collector, Marian talks about You, as if she knows You. Can

I know You? I want to communicate and be known by You too!

Marian starts talking to the Tear Collector.

"Now Tear Collector, help my heart. I miss my daughter so much."

She begins to share a story.

"His presence is like a blanket of peace resting on me when I miss my daughter. He heals my heart."

"Wow, I love that, I want my own heart to heal and experience peace, too."

Marian continues, "When my daughter died, He comforted me and gathered my tears. He alleviated the pain in my heart through my most difficult moments."

I see peace fill her eyes.

"He sends peace to encompass me and makes it tangible."

I sit with big eyes and my jaw wide while her words settle in my heart. She takes a deep breath.

"I rest and He gives rest to my body and peace to my mind. He talks to me."

"I didn't know He could talk to you. I would like comfort from my losses, too." I say with my head hung low.

Marian assures me, "You can have conversations with the Tear Collector, too. He is trying to talk to you. Tune in, He is speaking."

I don't hear You though, do I? I've never met anyone like Marian. She believes what You tell her. Help me tune in to Your voice, I want to hear You.

I continue asking Marian questions.

"How can I hear the Tear Collector speak?"

"Honey, He is always speaking," she replies. "Awareness is key. First, you must be aware He is communicating with you. You just don't know it."

"I hear nothing though."

Marian continues, "Do you want to encounter the Tear Collector on the Other Side?"

"What do you mean *the Other Side*?"

"It's the spiritual realm, where the Facets of His heart reside. You can hear and see in the spiritual realm. You enter by love and you see His perspective," she says confidently.

I am standing next to her sofa. I repeat her words to myself, "You can hear and see the spiritual realm. Yes, I want that. I want to see His perspective."

With tears moving down my cheeks, the doorbell rings.

"Excuse me, dear. I'll be right back," she hands me a box of tissue and moves towards the door.

I hear Marian say," Well hello! It's good to see you again, thank you, I will give this to her."

She sits down on the L-shaped sofa again and hands me a box. "You have a very special delivery today."

I'm perplexed, "But no one knows I'm here."

"Honey, the guardian knows you are here, and she says it's time."

"Time for what?"

"God has heard your cries and sees your tears and wants you to discover the heart of God. Are you ready, Sandy?"

"Yes, I want to know Him!"

I open the box and discover a master crafted key lying in velvet. The bow of the key is set with a faceted heart and a crown adorning the top.

"This key unlocks your heart. Once unlocked, your heart will begin to meet the different Facets of God. Place it on your heart and tell Him your desires."

I'm hesitant. Will I look foolish speaking to no one? I place the key next to my heart and close my eyes and decide to speak from my heart.

"God, I want to know the Facets of Your heart. I want to hear Your voice. Please speak to me in ways I know it's You. I want to know who You are, Tear Collector."

I open my eyes.

"Stretch out your hands to receive Him, and say, 'Tear Collector, submerge me in Your love.'"

"I want someone to validate my tears. I want to know Your love so badly."

I slowly extend my hands, palms open to encounter Your love. My heart's desires continue.

"Submerge me in Your comfort and peace, Tear Collector. I want to hear You speak."

I repeat it.

"I want to hear You speak!" I exclaim.

I feel a wave of love and peace cascade over me. I can't believe what I'm feeling. I start to hear unknown words. Marian stands next to me, her hands rest on my shoulder.

"Are you hearing any words? He will give you words and it might seem strange or unfamiliar, but just say them out loud."

The words fumble out of my mouth. "Bellisimo tushtarde squisanana bellismo."

Marian asks the Tear Collector, "What are You trying to tell Sandy?"

She begins to write the interpretation. "My daughter you are altogether beautiful and perfect."

My heart expands. I can hear the Tear Collector's gentle words. He speaks to me! I can hear Him! "Tear Collector, thank You for making room in my heart. You pushed aside my hurt and pain with Your love and for once I feel calm. Your love transforms from a mere thought to an entire movement in my heart. Your love feels like a warm fuzzy blanket encircling me. I feel You carrying me to a place of refuge; it's Your heart. You've made a place in my heart full of trust, I finally feel I can trust someone."

I'm relaxed, I feel like I've been soaking in a hot bath. I feel calm, clean, and at peace. It's the first time I encounter peace. I hear the Tear Collector speak again assuring me,

I will never leave you! I'm always here to comfort you.

The good news overtakes me, but a heaviness still weighs on my chest. My broken relationships start to overwhelm me.

"Wait, are You sure You won't leave me?"

The uncertainty concerns me.

"People say a lot of things to me and their words always fail, their words fall to the ground."

I am not a liar. I mean what I say.

"I've had many people leave," I say in disappointment. "People I love are absent from my life: Mom, Mercy, Victoria, my biological father. I don't want to see the people I love leave me anymore."

I will be here. I want to comfort you with My love. My love is deep and wide, and immeasurable by your sight. It's powerful enough to go into your deepest pain and memories and remove something never meant to be there. I created you to be brave. I want you to trust Me. Will you come with Me on a memory journey? I want to take you to the memory of your house fire. I want to comfort you on the day you face the ashes.

The Tear Collector takes my hand and welcomes me to the Other Side.

We're in a familiar living room, we're in the house on Black Diamond Trail. I see a spark ignite into a moving flame from the electrical outlet adjacent to the Christmas tree. The fire engulfs the Christmas lights and tinsel, melting our family ornaments. The fire is hungry, the more it eats, the bigger it becomes, doubling, tripling in size, engulfing everything in its path. Thick black smoke hugs the ceiling, coiling through the living room and into the kitchen. The wallpaper shrinks and curls, feeding the fire.

I'm afraid, but I'm not coughing, I'm not hot. I'm holding onto the Tear Collector and my heart breaks for myself, my family, and my childhood home.

"I can't look at it anymore, Tear Collector. I can't watch this home burn."

The Tear Collector listens, and we move outside. The fire is extinguished. We're standing on the edge of an ash pit. All of my belongings, everything valuable to me, no longer exists. The tears start to fall. Each tear holds tiny words. Erin's hope chest, Jody Dog, Kat, my houe, Strawberry Shortcake bedspread, Garfield stuffed animal. Each word slides off my warm cheeks. The Tear Collector's finger touches my cheek and gathers all my word-filled tears.

Each of your tears are a treasure to Me. I collect them in this vase.

My tears continue to fall: Home, Mom's art, Dad's guitar, Fear of Homelessness, Love, Forgiveness, Loneliness. I gaze down at the smoking ashes and the Tear Collector gently places my hand in His.

I've collected these tears, I've kept track of all your sorrows. I've collected your tears in My bottle. I have recorded each one in My book. I see you standing here brokenhearted. At this moment, I know what you need as an eight-year-old and as an adult. You need healing in these painful memories.

Again, my eyes fill up. I turn and grab the Tear Collector. His strong arms embrace my little frame. I feel protected. This is what I need. I've lacked comfort in my tragedies. The Tear Collector holds a beautiful pink vase in His hand. It's full of my tears. He gently touches my tears and moves them to the bottle's opening.

I'm sorry you are hurting. I'm sorry you lost all of your pets, toys, and everything that mattered to you. It hurts Me when you hurt. These tragic tears are valuable to Me. I cherish them.

He opens His arms again and cradles me. I squeeze His neck with all I have. In His embrace, I cry a deep cry. I pull my face away from His shoulder and look at Him. I watch His eyes pool with tears.

I hurt when you hurt. Despite the Destroyer's plans for your life, Mine are greater. My love is more extravagant than the destruction. I will bring beauty from these ashes. Let Me take those tears. They are precious. It's important to cry. Tears cleanse and free your soul. I designed your body to heal. The shedding of tears is part of this process. I gather your tears. I have collected every single tear you have ever shed, and I store them in the Remembrance Room. I want to show you how much I value what you've gone through, let's go there now and you will see that everything important to you is important to Me.

I take in His words. I let them consume me and I begin to surrender my pain to Him.

"I've felt so much heartache. I've felt forgotten and unloved."

I want you to know that you matter. Everything you've been through matters.

Stepping into the room, I see a beautiful prism. I smell an intoxicating citrus fragrance. There is a beautiful radiant light hitting the angles of glass, creating tiny and enormous rainbows dancing throughout the room.

Beveled glass shelves in the shape of gems fill the room. Placed on each shelf are beautiful vases of all sizes and colors and every one of them has a label:

Sandra's Birthday
Skinned Knee 1979
Teeth Through Lip
Erin's Death
House Fire
Mother's Life

They continue: Driving Home Alone From Wedding, Sleeping Alone, Throwing Garden Shovel at Ankle, Mom Spanked Sandy, Chopping Lettuce Wrong, No Perfect Attendance Certificate, Dad and Mom Fighting, Roy Isn't Your Biological Father.

I designed each one of these vases from the broken pieces of your life. Aren't they all beautiful when you see them together in one room? Every tragic experience you've grieved is in this room. Every vase is uniquely different and each one contains the tears you shed during the moment. Tears are significant. They are the entry point to your heart healing. Tears break the ground for healing to begin in the heart. In My Letters I share, 'Blessed are those who mourn for they will be comforted.' It's important to mourn your losses.

I want to bring redemption into your life so you can show others the way too. I want to display your broken pieces from this vase and show you I can redeem them by bringing healing to your heart. I want to redeem pieces of your life you don't value, or you think are too painful to revisit. I want to show you beauty in the broken pieces of your life. I value each broken piece. I don't want you to forget the pain you've endured.

The Tear Collector points to a beautiful vase.

See this vase?

It's large and iridescent and stands in the center of the room.

It holds all the tears I've shed for you.

My hand slides along the vase.

"I had no idea."

I want you to know how much I value what you've endured and experienced. Your life is precious to Me and I'm going to show you on our journey how I will use all of your tears. I have something special I want to do with them at a later time. The Tear Collector nudges me. *In the near future you will be moving back to Iowa. However, I have someone I want you to meet on the Other Side. His name is Wall Shaker, and He can help with some things going on within your heart.*

I look around. Marian's living room surrounds me again. My cheeks are wet with tears, Marian offers a tissue and a place on her sofa.

"Thank you, Marian. Thank you for everything this afternoon. I'm so grateful for the introduction to the Tear Collector. I already feel lighter. I feel more at peace and full of love. I need to go home to my kids, thank you. I will see you soon."

Marian hugs me and walks me to the door.

"Honey, I know there is so much He wants to do in your heart. I will hide and watch," she says with a smile.

I turn and wave, walking back to my house. I pull the faceted key out of my pocket. Captivated, I smile, I'm ready to meet the Wall Shaker.

The Facets

Chapter 9

WALL SHAKER

"...For God who said, 'Let brilliant light shine out of darkness,' is the One who has cascaded His light into us – the brilliant dawning light of the glorious knowledge of God as we gaze into the face of Jesus Christ."
~ 2 Corinthian 4:5 TPT

I smile at my kids and pull the minivan door shut.

"I think that's everything!" I yell to Josh, putting his luggage in the trunk of his car.

We are ready for the journey to Iowa. I feel a small reluctance to move back. Iowa reminds me of my mother's death, and I want to leave it behind me. Josh graduated from college and will work for the Federal Aviation Administration in Cedar Rapids, of all places. He sent his resume throughout the country and he lands a job in Iowa. I never wanted to move back nor did I think we ever would. But as life evolves, I want to be closer to my brother's family and have Sunday dinners together. His twin daughters are three months younger than my daughter, Karis. I hope our kids can be close.

When we arrive, we'll stay at the Dellamuth's while we house hunt. Michelle Dellamuth is a high school friend and a roommate at one time. We spent nights in their basement singing, dancing, and watching movies. They feel like a second family to me and I'm grateful to see them again after all these years.

Josh will drive his car, and I've got the kids. I turn on the engine, look in the rearview mirror, and smile seeing my kids all buckled in the car seats. Joshua, or JJ as we call him is five years old; he is a responsible big brother with a golden heart. Karis is three, chatty and sassy. She'll be a heartbreaker when she's older. Kingston sits and smiles with a twinkle in his blue eyes. He's part koala, always holding tight to my limbs. I remember at three months he learned to latch on and hug for dear life, I can't believe that was five months ago. I turn around to face the kids for a quick prayer before our journey.

"Okay, let's pray you guys. God, protect us on our trip to Iowa. Amen."

"Amen," they all repeat in unison.

Driving isn't my favorite way to spend Mother's Day, but it will be an exciting move to be closer to family.

Ten minutes after pulling out of the driveway, Kingston's bottle falls to the floor and he won't stop crying. I call Josh.

"We need to pull over, I can't reach Kingston's bottle."

We skirt over to the roadside and I put it back in his hands.

JJ then exclaims, "I need to pee!"

Josh maneuvers to the red dirt ditch and JJ nervously starts urinating.

"Are you doing okay, Josh?" His eyes are red, and he looks sleepy.

"I'll be fine, I'm tired from the Alaska flight."

His guard unit returned from a mission the night before. He looks tired, but we need to arrive in Iowa soon because he starts work on Monday.

"Okay, I want to make sure you are okay to drive."

"I'll be fine," he reassures me.

We are back on the road, and another thirty minutes pass. Karis tells me with her little raspy voice that she needs to pee.

"Oh Karis!" I say in frustration.

This may be the last car ride I'll ever take with these three. Traveling with three kids under 5 years old is not for the faint of heart. I call Josh again.

"We need to pull over at the next gas station so Karis can go to the bathroom."

I feel uneasy at the gas station. Something is not right, when I return to the car, I ask the kids to pray with me.

"This is a difficult start to a long drive, let's all pray again. God, help us get to Iowa safely. Have your angels surround the vehicles and the tires. Please help the kids be content on the road. Amen!"

Returning to the road, we drive for another hour and the kids want food. I call Josh.

"The kids are hungry, we need to pull over."

"There's a restaurant off the Tuttle/Newcastle exit, follow me."

He hangs up and we exit I-44. We wind through the two-lane highway for what feels like forever. I wonder if I should call Josh. This is far from the interstate. What is he doing? I don't want to be a nag. I'll be quiet, I'm sure we are almost there.

Right before my eyes, Josh slowly turns into oncoming traffic, pauses, then fulfills the turn and hits a woman in an SUV. BAM! I see Josh's trunk pop open, the luggage he packed hours before flies out. His car slides into the ditch kicking up loose gravel from the side of the road. Josh's car pushes the woman's SUV into the ditch, causing her air bag to go off. I silently scream, wondering if he's dead.

Quickly, I park the van on the shoulder of the highway.

"Kids, mommy will be right back."

I race across the highway to see if Josh is alive. His eyes are squinting and groggy. Thank God! He looks as though he just woke up. Another driver pulls over and offers to help.

Josh is holding his ankle.

"I think I dislocated it."

It looks like a wet noddle, dangling in his hands.

"No, I think you broke it. What happened?!" I scream.

"I guess I fell asleep because the next thing I know, the car crashed."

I pace with my hand on my forehead wondering what to do. A stranger brings me to the side of the road.

"I just checked on the woman, she is shaken but she is okay, are you okay?" He looks at me, waiting for a reply.

I don't understand what he's saying. There is a momentary high pitch buzzing in my ear. Finally, he says it really slow.

"Is there someone you can call to help you?"

"Yes, I'll call my husband's friend John, he lives near here, in Oklahoma City."

I flip my phone open and dial John,

"John, Josh was in an accident!" I cry.

"Is he okay?"

"I don't know."

"Do you know where you are?"

"I don't know."

"Do you know where they will take him?"

"I don't know."

"Can you stay where you are?"

"Yes, I can do that."

John talks in a soothing voice, for a moment I feel calm.

"Can I talk to someone who knows where you are at?"

"Yes," I reply and I hand the phone to the first responder who answers John's questions.

Another stranger comes up to me.

"Ma'am you need to get yourself together, you have kids. Be strong for your kids." Her words snap me out of shock.

I run over to check on my kids as the ambulance pulls up. I slide the van door open.

"Kids, Daddy was in an accident, it looks like he broke his ankle, but he will be okay. The ambulance will drive him to the hospital, and you will play at John's house, while I go check on Daddy."

I sit in the ER, staring at the brick wall, waiting for the doctor to release Josh. I look around at the other people waiting and wonder if they have suffered as much tragedy as I have in my thirty years of life. The wall begins to shake as a man walks through the bricks that appear solid, but it's a portal. I blink my eyes, and I find myself on the Other Side.

The Wall Shaker introduces himself,

I'm glad to meet you Sandy, looks like your Mother's Day isn't going so great.

"No, it's not Wall Shaker! I'm a magnet for attracting bad things in my life. This accident being the latest in a list of bad things. Can I be up front with You? When will the next bad thing happen? I think I've been through enough. When will things turn around? Goodness, this world is dangerous. I'm scared to drive, worried some other driver will fall asleep at the wheel. I want protection. I don't want to get hurt anymore!"

Sandy, this would have a much different ending if you hadn't prayed. Your prayers are powerful and effective. You called angels around the car an hour earlier. Remember when Josh paused before they collided? Had he not paused, it would have been a head on collision. You weren't on the Interstate. If he would have fallen asleep going 75 mph there would be a tragic ending today.

"You're right, I did have a sense something was wrong an hour before the accident," I admitted.

You've witnessed the power of prayer. Whenever you feel something, anything at all, always remember to give Your concerns to me, He replied.

"I understand, but sometimes it's easier to build this protective wall around myself. I can remove myself from people. I can remove myself from memories, my husband and the accident, my mom's death, my kids. Do you see these walls I've erected? I can't get hurt behind them. I've been building my own fortress for years."

The Wall Shaker knocks on the bricks.

Do you feel protected? Are you still as motivated when you first started building?

"No, I'm not nearly as motivated. I'm unable to move higher or go wider. I'm unable to see, or feel, or move. I'm actually getting worn out."

Wow, that's quite the job for one person. Why are you the only one building the fortress?

"I don't want to invite someone else into this place. It's for me and me alone. I want a place in my heart that doesn't hurt, a place where I feel safe, a place I can build the life I want. I want a fortress that allows me the freedom to go anywhere and do what I want and not feel pain."

I continue to share my story with the Wall Shaker.

"My mother's unresolved murder hurts. Josh, Jerry, my brother - I'm building my walls to protect myself from these people. I'm afraid of Jerry. He's estranged from the family and isolated my sisters from me and the rest of our family. We're the only family they knew, and we were gone in one day.

"Josh is angry. I feel I can't do anything right anymore. I don't keep the house clean. I'm tired of picking up the kids' toys and cooking meals. It's never good enough. I don't feel supported and it's crushing." I go on, "I'm done with everyone's passive aggressive digs directed at me. I give people too much credit. I actually believe them when they promise something. I believe them when they say they'll follow through. Then I become disappointed, but disappointment is my own fault, right? It's my own problem, they say. It's my responsibility for breaking relationships they say. Nope, I'm not a fan, that's why I'm building this fortress."

I let out a deep sigh.

Who told you to build a fortress? Who told you to keep everyone out?

"My own pain told me I could protect myself if I built walls."

Pain distorts, He advises.

"Besides, when I'm busy building I don't think about painful thoughts, disappointing myself, or disappointing others. It's my way of controlling the situation. They can't hurt me if I have walls surrounding me. I'm determined to finish my building project, but then Josh comes along and discourages me. He tells me, 'It's never going to work. You don't finish anything you start. Can you finish something for once?' These words motivate me to work harder and faster."

Do you know why words of discouragement cause the acceleration? He asks.

"Why?"

Words are catalysts. They are magnets, drawing emotional feelings to them. Words are powerful. I want you to know the power of your own words. Words create. Can I share something with you? Do you know how you are building this fortress?

"How?" Now I'm intrigued.

You're not building with your hands, you're building with your thoughts. You create bricks with your thoughts. Those bricks are filled with the Destroyer's thoughts. However, bricks are made of particles of sand and My thoughts of you are grains of sand. Each of My wonderful thoughts of you are tiny particles you can't see with the naked eye. One brick is made of millions of my thoughts. The thoughts you put together, build a life and a mentality. Are you going to create a life with My thoughts? Or are you going to create a life with the Destroyer's thoughts? Which will you make your own?

Distrust erects these walls. Deep down you erect these walls to keep Me out because you don't trust Me. Let's go to this place of pain that built this wall between you and Me. Are you tired of living in torment?

"Yes, I want out. This place of torment is overtaking me. I'm deceived, I thought it was a place of protection but it's lonely. I can't escape the lies I've built around myself. My walls are too tall. But what about my family? What if they don't believe Your thoughts of me? What if they don't see me the way You see me?"

You're right. It's true, they might not.

A military cannon full of iridescent light strikes the wall and pieces fall to the floor. A thrust of shiny champagne colored dust moves like confetti in the air.

I want to shed light on some things inside your heart.

"I don't know about that. I'm not sure I want to see the hurt, disappointment, and brokenness in my heart."

Sandy, I know it's hard and uncomfortable, but I want you to trust Me in this moment. Will you let Me show you?

He reaches His hand out. I scrunch my eyes and slowly reach out my hand.

Open your eyes, Sandy. Blow the illuminating dust on the wall and tell me what you see.

Taking the shiny dust off the floor, I blow it from my hand to the wall. I'm startled by my surroundings. No wonder I'm unable to move, I realize I'm surrounded by three concrete walls with erratic writing. Bars define the fourth wall.

"I'm not building a fortress. I'm building a… prison??" My face freezes in disbelief.

You are. This is a prison of lies. First, it was a grain of sand, a strategic lie of the Destroyer, a thought fortified with emotion and mortared with denial. Recognizing and acknowledging the truth will remove these walls. However, it is your choice. This prison is impenetrable. You can only dismantle the prison from the inside, because you're the one who knows how it's built.

"But how did I get here? Why aren't You helping me get out?" I plead.

The question isn't why am I not helping, but why do you stay? I gave you everything you need to get yourself out. Believe My words! In My Letters I tell you, you can demolish every deceptive fantasy that opposes Me and break through every arrogant attitude raised up in defiance of the true knowledge of God. We capture, like prisoners of war, every thought and insist it bows in obedience to the Anointed One.

I pose the questions, "Aren't You all powerful? Aren't You all knowing? What if I don't want to leave because I don't know anything else?"

I am powerful. But your self-wisdom and choices are canceling My will for you. I know all things, including the motives of hearts.

I know how you see yourself. I know how you see Me. I know everything but I don't take action on how you think I should move. Plus, I value freedom and I gave you the authority to choose. You need to want to leave your own prison, I can't do it for you.

"Don't You think I want out?"

Well, to get out, you will have to remove deceit.

"What? I don't think I'm being deceived."

That's the thing about deceit, it's not detectable. You are in deceit and you are in denial about your feelings of Me. You resist what's best for you. Let's talk about your mom.

Anger boils inside of me and I yell, "Wall Shaker, I'm angry! I'm angry she was murdered. I'm enraged that someone didn't value her and intentionally took her life. She consistently put herself in unhealthy relationships. She made so many poor choices in her life. I'm mad she slept with Jerry, but then again, I'm not sure we could have reconciled without the twins."

I continue with rage, "There hasn't been an arrest! it's irritating! I can't believe the years I've lived without her and justice still hasn't been served. I've submerged myself in being a detective to solve her murder. I'm frustrated! In my naiveté, I did not realize the justice system is so broken. I built walls to protect myself from my own family. I didn't realize it, but many things in my heart are missing from her absence in my life. I replaced my hopes, dreams and happiness with trauma, confusion, and disillusion. That moment defined me. The end of her life was the beginning of my hopelessness! Don't You care about justice? Why hasn't there been anything done about my mom's murder case? A murderer walks free as we've waited for an arrest!!"

The anger continues to spew out of me.

"Did You even care about her? It feels like You left me alone to figure it out."

Resentment fills me.

"Wall Shaker, how do I know You cared about her?"

She is with Me, and I was with her when she died.

I freeze. The anger and resentful thoughts leave.

"What?! How can this be? I don't even know if she owned a copy of the Letters."

Do you want Me to show you?

"Of course," I declare.

The Wall Shaker shows me my mother. She's on the Other Side sitting by a fountain! I can tell she is free! She looks happy and joyful. The stresses of life aren't weighing her down anymore.

"Wall Shaker, how can it be?" I say shaking my head.

A memory runs through my mind. When I went through her belongings after her death, I found a letter I had written her four years earlier, telling her about Jesus.

Yes, she read the letter and wanted Me. She wanted the Tear Collector to acknowledge and heal the pain she had been through in her life. I showed her I was with her every time she cried.

"Fifteen years after her death, and I didn't think she was with You! I believed a lie for years. This changes everything." I'm in utter shock, "I thought she was forever separated from You, in hell. She dabbled with New Age, there was a guru in Florida, alternative idols, yet I know she was always searching. I assumed I'd never see her again."

This news crashes into my heart, "I'm elated I get to see her again! How did I believe this lie?"

The lie entered your heart when you judged her. You based your thoughts of her on lies, even the same lies she believed about herself. Judgement causes numbness to the heart. I set aside part of your heart for people, but judgement hinders your clarity of seeing them how I see them. It causes part of your heart to malfunction. I created you to love with your heart, not use your heart to judge those whom you love. You invited Me into your life at eleven years old. How long did it take from the moment on Newport Beach until now before anyone would know you are My daughter?

"Probably, over a decade," I reply.

Did it change the truth that you were My daughter? Your mother had four years. She always looked for truth just like you, even if it didn't look 'religious'. There isn't a man-made check list I require for people to follow Me.

"I am relieved to learn You were with her when she died, and to know she wasn't alone in her final moments. I want to tell her some things. Please let me. Can we freeze the moment before she died? I want her to leave the earth full of love."

Yes, we can. Are you sure about this? It will be difficult.

"Yes, I want one more chance. I want one more time to look in her blue eyes, to see her face. I want to see her as she is now, in Heaven. I want to be fully engaged and, in the moment, not thinking of anything else. I've always wanted just one more time to talk to her."

There's a flash, another brilliant burst of champagne dust, and when my eyes re-adjust, I see her sitting in her favorite blue swivel recliner. Her back is facing the front door. I grab the Wall Shaker's hand as we stand in the same room as my mom.

"Mom," I whisper.

My body starts to tremble. Tears flow from my eyes. Here is my heart's desire. I've wanted to talk to her and now I get my chance. I have all these mixed emotions jumping inside of me. I am elated to see her. I'm sad this will be the last time in my lifetime. I see her face look at me. Her bright blue eyes gaze into mine.

"Oh, Mom!" I run over to her chair and hold her, not

wanting to let her go. It feels so good to touch her, to smell her patchouli perfume with a hint of stale smoke, a scent I once hated and now long for.

"I've missed you so much! So much has happened since you've been gone. I have a family and a husband. I own a business. Jason had twins, too, and they look like you! Mercy and Victoria aren't in my life. I'm so sorry Mom, I know I let you down. I know you wanted me to take care of them if anything happened to you, but I failed. I didn't get to be a part of their lives but I love them and pray for them."

Mom seems rattled, "I don't understand. I'm confused. What is going on?"

"I know this doesn't make sense right now." As I continue, she looks over at the Wall Shaker. Her eyes fixate on Him and she is captivated.

Mom asks, "Why are you and the Wall Shaker here?"

"In the next moment Wall Shaker will remove the wall between you and Heaven, but first I want to share my heart with you. I want you to know I love you so much! I am so thankful you were chosen to be my mother."

I continue to share my heart with her.

"You are a beautiful person. You are not only beautiful on the outside, but your heart radiates with beauty; you love your family, you love your friends. I found your old letters to those you loved. You expressed your love for me in journals and I never knew how strong your love is for me. You shared your frustration and hurt when I was a teenager. I didn't acknowledge your pain and I'm so sorry I hurt you. I allowed my pain of your struggles to hinder me from seeing who you really are. You are beautiful. His creation is perfect. I can see that now. You are so creative, expressing your feelings in writing, color, and shapes. Your heart bled for so many years. I long to be creative like you and express it in my own life. I am honored you are my mother. I'm sorry I didn't honor you like I should have, but now I can see you clearly. I'm sorry for all the hurtful things I've said in the past. When you struggled with betrayal, death, and depression, and I acted like you were dead. I am so sorry for my words and actions. Please forgive me."

I want to hold her, I want to cry in her arms.

"I've experienced what life is like without you. Many times, I want to call and ask for your advice or call to hear your voice. I will miss you. I did not understand how much your absence would affect my life. The other day I found the blessing you wrote me when I turned eighteen. It was in the last Christmas card you sent. I treasure it! Your words melted into my heart. My soul longed for those words for many years, I'm so glad you wrote them down as I continue to re-read them.

"I've been numb for so long I don't allow myself to cry because I don't think the tears will stop. I built a wall around myself. A few years ago, when a friend came into my life, she saw that I never mourned your death. Finally, I allowed myself to mourn your loss. Some days out of the blue, I allow myself to cry and acknowledge I still miss you. I wish your life didn't have to end like this. I wish I could have you longer. I know He has His hands around you and is loving you. I will see you on the Other Side. I will see you in Heaven. You are one of the first people I want to see when I get there. Please greet me!"

I nod at the Wall Shaker. I then see a beautiful white light release love onto her. The wall between Heaven and Earth is removed. The barrier is gone. We're standing in her room and I can feel the beauty, I can see new life, I can feel freedom.

Wall Shaker asks her if she's ready to leave.

"Yes," she smiles.

In this moment, she becomes His. I sense her heart long

for Him. He satisfied her heart. In all my life, I had never seen her as satisfied as she is now. He scoops her up and carries her away. He delivers her from the future trauma. I see Him remove her before the fatal blows.

"Thank You for delivering her to Heaven. Thank You for taking her before her body experienced violence. Thank You for showing me the goodness of who You are. Thank You for caring and rescuing her."

I want you to take comfort in knowing she is more alive than you. Love never fails. It never ends. Her love for you is alive. She is part of the great cloud of witnesses cheering you on.

We leave her trailer and return to my fortress of lies.

I sit in silence on the dirt floor of my self-made prison. I process the heart changing moment. I allow the new truths to saturate my heart. I see the judgments I've made about my mother — how she lived her life without understanding the pain she sustained. I didn't have compassion for her. She created her own fortress of lies and I judged her for them.

The Destroyer loves to lie to us in places of trauma and pain. The heartache from her relationship with her dad, parenting guilt, the death of Erin, the house fire, betrayal from loved ones, losing her parents. It's impossible to have a fulfilled heart when you don't process pain. You are doing what your mother didn't.
She has prayed you would process the pain.

"I'm sorry for judging You as uncaring and ignorant, Wall Shaker. I've been so angry and disillusioned. I've held grudges and bitterness towards You. Please forgive me for judging You, for putting You in a box, when in actuality I limited and boxed in myself."

I understand you. You were trying to protect yourself. However, you kept Me and those you love out. You judged others without thinking much about their personal situations. You may think judgements don't affect you however, judgements about one person or a group of people isolate you. Multiple judgments create prisons and fortresses built upon pride, bitterness, and resentment, adding bricks to this prison. You will help others take them down, you will be a wall shaker for other people.

"Yes, I want people to know who You are and what You can do with their hearts! I will shake everything that can be shaken," I declare.

When hearts are healed, prison walls come down. My children will live free and release those in prison.

"Thank You for revealing Your goodness in my darkest moment."

I want you to know your darkest moment was your mother's brightest moment.

The Wall Shaker takes my hand. *Look at Me.*

In the next moment, the walls shake violently. One by one they begin to fall. Nothing is standing between us anymore. He shows me The Promised Land. At the top of the mountain, there's a valley filled with purple, red, blue, and yellow wildflowers as far as the sunset. There is a sweet fragrance of orange blossoms and white lilies in the air.

I'm taking you to The Promised Land, there is ground to occupy.

I look up and see Josh on crutches exiting the ER. I help him to the car and we slowly pull out of the hospital parking lot.

"How are you feeling, Josh?"

He looks over at me, "I'm kind of out of it. Hey, you have

some dust or something on your shoulder. Let me get it off."

I look down and see a shimmer of champagne dust on my shoulder. He brushes it off and rolls down his window. We watch the tiny particles fly into the wind, over the interstate and into the clouds.

Chapter 10

WEAVER

So we are convinced that every detail of our lives is continually woven together to fit into God's perfect plan of bringing good into our lives, for we are his lovers who have been called to fulfill his designed purpose.

~ *Romans 8:28 TPT*

Moving boxes are scattered throughout our new house. I'm excited for this fresh start in Iowa. Josh takes JJ to run errands, leaving the two younger kids with me. As they settle down for their afternoon nap, I begin to unpack the linen closet boxes.

A variety of blankets, towels, sheets, and pillowcases stuff each box. I find a baby afghan buried beneath a set of bathroom towels. I hold it in my hands, running my fingers over the pattern. I look up and notice the Weaver standing in my hallway. With love-filled eyes, the Weaver brings something forward from behind His back. He's holding a small object.

Sandy, I want to show you something.

He slowly opens his hands and I see a half-finished baby rattle. My eyes become big.

"Oh yes, I remember that," I reply. A wave of sadness comes over me.

"My Grandma and I made Erin a baby rattle. I remember snuggling up to my grandma as she placed the little gold bell inside the rattle. We used green yarn to sew it all together."

Why didn't you finish it?

"Well, Erin died before we could finish it."

Did you want to finish it?

I think to myself that I did want to finish it. I remember being upset when my grandma stopped the project.

"I was four years old, I don't know if I understood what was happening," I say.

I want to show you how I weave and resolve. This may be a hard thing for you because it doesn't resemble what you think. If I take the yarn from the rattle and weave it into something else, it has the original beauty from your heart, from your grandmother and sister, and I will make something beautiful from it. When you give Me things that concern you, I can bring resolve them. Most times, it will not look like what you think. I may re-purpose it, revise, or revive it, and it will be more beautiful than you can ever imagine. When people give Me permission to move in their lives, I will make all things new again. So, let's start with this afghan.

"Wow, that's a glorious mess!" I laugh.

The afghan is vibrant with life, yet there are big holes and a mismatched, incomplete pattern.

This is your life in color and yarn. When your mother was pregnant with you, I knit you in her womb. Even before you were born, I made plans and created purpose for you.

If people let Me into their lives, I can turn things around. I can bring resolution. I can take the broken pieces, the unraveled parts of our lives, even the holes, and I can re-stitch them. See this glistening gold thread? That's Me weaving throughout your life. These are the parts you have granted Me access to weave. I want to show you a bigger picture. Let's go beyond this.

I see my afghan connecting with other afghans. I see the glistening threads zipping through my afghan through others' rainbow threads creating bigger, more beautiful afghans. I start to see my work on earth, connecting other hearts with His heart. I notice my afghan has similar patterns to the others.

"What does that mean, Weaver?"

You've had similar situations in your lives. Those patterns are common ground you share. Here, let's look deeper.

Before my eyes, I see the entire world. An afghan covers every inch. Billions of afghans connect to each other creating one world-size afghan covering oceans, rivers, deserts, and mountains. This afghan brings comfort to the world.

You play a part in the world, making a difference, affecting many people. Everyone plays their own part in the world. The more you allow Me to resolve in your life, the more your heart will feel peace and healing. Your reach goes further. I connect more hearts when you are connected to Mine, and I can take glistening gold threads and weave beauty into every place. Let's get back to your very own afghan. Now I've given you a vision of what can happen when we take care of the holes, fraying patterns, and too much yarn. Sometimes to move forward we must look back. See this wayward pattern? We need to unravel it. This is part of your thinking that I want to re-knit. This will affect the whole blanket; how you look forward and how you look back.

"Unravel it?" I ask, "Won't that mess with everything else? That takes so much time and why mess with the good things in my life?"

Some things are beautiful and not perfect, and that is My creation. Other things need to be fixed to make the connection and add to a bigger afghan. However, you have a choice. You don't have to unravel anything. What are you thinking?

A thought pops into my head and I quickly respond,

"Well, unraveling sounds like it will emotionally hurt. I don't know if I'm prepared for that."

You know how it can be a challenge for you to pinpoint your feelings?

I think about my relationship with Josh.

"You're right, I do. When Josh and I talk, I have the hardest time telling him how I really feel about a situation. I'm afraid he will pull away when I'm vulnerable. I worry he won't be able to handle my feelings. I worry he will leave me."

I continue to share my heart with the Weaver.

"Then there's my mother's death. Several times I struggle to find words to communicate my thoughts at the Johnson County Sheriff's station. When I learned my mother was murdered, I just sat there uttering the only words I could, 'So there is a murderer out there'?"

When your feelings don't have a voice, your emotions become bound. You limit your emotions to anger or sadness. You are afraid of what others will say or think if you share your true thoughts. You value their feelings over yours.

I begin to think of all my past and present relationships.

"It's true, I doubt myself. I might share my feelings and then worry I'll be rejected. What if I assume the wrong person murdered my mother? What if law enforcement goes after the wrong person? Are You saying I don't value my thoughts enough to freely express how I feel?"

Sandy, you can't manage people's emotions. It's not your place and it will wear you out. Besides, I will love you no matter how you feel or what you think.

I look up at the Weaver.

"Really? Don't You want me to think how You think?" I ask.

Since I already know your thoughts, I want you to invite Me into your situations. Ask Me, 'Weaver, what are you doing in this situation? Show me truth.' You can have as much truth as you want. I want you to share your emotions with Me. I want you to see situations from My heart. They are full of love, not fear or anger. I want the invitation to move into your heart and share truth. The only way to do this is to bring Me into the moment of pain, sadness, or anger. I want you to acknowledge those emotions and then process them. Don't camp out in the emotion for months or suppress them. Tough emotions can point to a wound. I want to heal the wounds. The way into the wound is through emotions, and if they are bound you will be stuck.

I look at the afghan again and notice the gold thread.

"Show me a wound that's bound with emotion."

The Weaver takes me on a memory journey to the morning of my mom's death. We are on the rusty stairs leading to my mom's trailer. I see Jerry and he assures me I'll see the twins again. Afraid of confronting him and asking him questions about the night of her death, I clam up. I become speechless. I don't want to upset him, so I give him what he wants; the girls. I lose my sisters because I'm afraid of upsetting my mother's lying, irresponsible ex-boyfriend.

My life has become a collection of appeasing others, walking on egg shells, and managing other people's feelings so I can continue a relationship with them, hoping to connect with them and find the connection I'm always searching for.

"I'm starting to see it now. I long for connection, but never share my thoughts because I don't want people to pull away. I don't express how I really feel to anyone, not even to my husband and friends because I don't want to lose them."

Do you see this lie? You are already disconnected when you don't share who you really are. I made your emotions. They are a vibrant part of your life. I'm confident I will resolve things for you. I want to process pain with you. I want to show you how your emotions are a key to breaking through the pain. It's important to acknowledge what you're feeling. To deny how you feel about something is not valuing yourself. So, let's acknowledge how you felt when the twins' family wouldn't let you see the girls.

"It makes me angry. I loved the girls. I was in their lives and they were in mine. Jerry took them away. It hurts my heart and I know it would've broken hers. For months I attempted to see them. I played nice, but it didn't work and I wasn't valuing myself."

I hear you and I see you in that pain. Give the pain and the unresolved relationship with your sisters to Me. When you give things of value to Me, I cherish them. I know it's hard, but I will weave beauty and bring good from this heartbreaking situation, be patient.

"It's Yours, I don't want the pain anymore. Please remove the spot on my afghan where the bound emotions and pain live."

As soon as I give the Weaver the pain of bound emotions and the broken relationship with my sisters, my unraveling begins. A radiant unraveling of laughter starts in my core, this laughter delivers me from my darkest bound emotions.

Here is something for you in addition to the joy.

The Weaver hands me my mom's favorite afghan, the one my grandmother made for her. It's a mess, it's torn and in terrible shape. The Weaver gives me golden yarn and a crochet hook.

This is the yarn from Erin's rattle, I want you to weave it into your mom's afghan. I want you to turn this old blanket into something beautiful.

I take the afghan, gold yarn, and crochet hook, and sit down next to the linen closet. I begin to weave the glistening yarn through the holes and around the splatters on the tattered blanket. I begin to transform its color and pattern into a gold crown. I finish tying off the last piece and I walk into Karis' room and gently cover my sleeping daughter with my mom's favorite afghan.

Chapter 11

BAGGAGE TAKER

"Then David left his baggage in the care of the baggage keeper and ran to the battle line."

~1 Sam. 17:22 NKJV

"I am desperate for Your help. I do not want this sad soul anymore. I've experienced loss after loss. Abandonment after abandonment. Rejection after rejection. I am 36 years old and I'm a mess. I feel everyone close to me has chewed me up, spit me out, and betrayed me at my most vulnerable moments. I am damaging myself with my destructive thoughts. I want to die. I have a reoccurring vision: a wire wraps around my throat and it becomes tighter and tighter. It's no longer what others have done, but what I am doing to myself. I self-sabotage myself with my thoughts."

I tell myself, "You will suffer in this marriage. You are never going to amount to anything. You are ugly. You are fat. You will always be broken and needy. You should have called your mother the day she was murdered.

What kind of a daughter are you? You were a mistake, likely

a product of a weekend fling. What purpose do you have, Sandy?"

"I have been cruel to myself. I have not valued myself like You want me to. If a friend spoke the way I speak to myself, I would not keep her as a friend. I let lies guide me as my compass."

"I desire a full life, I want to experience joy. I want to enjoy my own company and others' companionship. I am ready to run away from this life of hurt and fear and experience all You have in store for me."

I go downstairs in the basement storage room to grab my weekend bag. I open the door and feel overwhelmed. How will I ever find it in this wall of luggage? I spot it on the top shelf shoved in between two other bags. Stretching from my tip toes I grab the loop with my fingertips. When I almost have it, an avalanche of luggage falls to the floor. Oh, my word, I have too much stuff. I need to remove these bags. Looking through the fallen baggage I see shoes. I follow the shoes to a man's face.

Sandy, I am the Baggage Taker. Although this is a mess, there are some things inside of your heart I want to remove. I call it heart baggage. The heart baggage you carry hinders your heart from living fully alive. I want you to stop filling them and collecting them. When you are ready for Me to take them, everything will change. You will receive what I have done for you, have for you, and hope for you. You will recognize joy! You will understand how to cope with pain. You will be renewed. Are you ready to remove the heart baggage? I take delight in revealing lies and setting you free from your false identities. I have called you by name. You are Mine! I love you just as you are. I accept you no matter where you're at. I want to see you thrive! You are not alone. I am with you, always.

I think to myself, "I am ready". I have carried and collected all the baggage on my journey. I have not removed anything.

I packed and dragged the bags throughout Iowa, Oklahoma, Arizona, and now they are beyond my ability to carry. They're too heavy. I cannot move them without bumping into people. My baggage affects others and hurts myself. I am so tired.

"I need help. I am ready to deal with them," I reply.

Oh, Darling, I have waited for this day! I never meant for you to carry these. My way is easy and not burdensome. You are a brave one. Here are three bags I want to show you: a lavendar, green, and shiny red one. Let's look inside. Let's start with this green one.

I see a green piece of luggage. It's beaten up. It has thick brown leather straps worn thin. It's bursting at the seams and it's falling apart. As I undo the leather straps, I feel how heavy it is.

This is the bag you picked up when your sister Erin died. I call this piece of baggage 'Snares and Hooks of the Soul'. This is a generational bag you picked up.

As I open the luggage, I see silver and rust. I see hooks and tools in disrepair. They've lost their shapes. Some hooks have speckles of rust. Some hooks are shiny. When I look closely, I see names written on the hooks: Shame and Condemnation.

"What are these, Baggage Taker?"

These hooks represent the snares of the Enemy. You have been carrying these around for too long. Remember, in the Letters I told you the Destroyer tries to take advantage of situations. It's important not to be ignorant of his schemes. He is a liar. He is not creative. He tells My people the same lies. The snares are weapons against your soul. The Destroyer's lies even snared the first couple on earth. I told Adam and Eve who I was, and who they were. I gave them their identities, missions and authorities. However, they listened to the Destroyer, and shame was a result. You picked up shame. When Erin died, extreme pain and loss came into your life. With the loss of Erin, your mother disconnected from you as she dealt with the pain. Her disconnection caused you to feel shame.

"Yes, it happened. I remember being nine years old, knocking on my mom's bedroom I tugged to open it, but she locked herself in her room."

"She hollered, 'I need to be left alone, I'm having a spell!' I stood there listening to her cry and thought to myself, but I'm still here."

"I felt ignored and unimportant. I felt flawed. My mom fixed her attention on Erin's death. It felt like she lost herself in what she didn't have instead of what she did have. She had me and Jason, Roy, and her parents. Wasn't I valuable to her? Couldn't she help me with my losses? Now, as a mother myself, I cannot imagine the grief of losing a child. Losing a seven-month-old baby to a congenital heart defect while in open-heart surgery would shatter my soul. Then, just a few years later, a house fire destroys everything. One of the most valuable and irreplaceable items lost in the fire was Erin's hope chest. Mom suffered so much loss. I suffered loss, too, but I never knew how to process our disconnection, so I blamed myself. "

"After these tragedies, I am desperate to connect with my mother. She isn't around so I seek attention from my father. Roy is busy working at the manufacturing plant, escaping his own pain. I need comfort from him too, but I do not find it. The identity of my biological father is still a mystery, I feel I have no one. When I'm alone, I suck my thumb and twirl my hair to comfort myself. My mother punishes my thumb sucking, soaking my fingers in smelly tinctures. Doesn't she know I need her? I need comfort and to be nurtured by her."

The snares and hooks bring condemnation and rejection. This is when the lies and false identities ensnare you. The lies 'You aren't good enough,' 'You're not valuable,' 'Your entire being isn't whole,' are seeds planted in your soul and they're all lies. Shame is another hook in your heart, and it tells you that you're unimportant and undeserving of love. It keeps you from seeing yourself the way I see you.

"How do You see me?"

You are bright and beautiful. You're talented and creative. You are perfect to Me.

"I know shame strips me of my positive self-image. I see the ripple effect in my life. I live in a cycle of shame, growing up in my family and recycling shame in my marriage. I grew up disconnected, so it became my normal understanding of living. My husband is a continuation of that pattern, connecting and disconnecting from me. I recognize it's harmful, and I feel unlovable. It feels like he values our relationship less than his other relationships. Instead of getting angry with him, I feel like I'm the problem. I feel like something is wrong with me and I wonder if that's why he sometimes turns to other opinions instead of mine.

The lies continue … if only I were prettier, skinnier, or funnier, then maybe Josh would love me more. Maybe he would be satisfied with me and not seek approval from other people. The lies grow deeper … if only I could contribute more financially to the family, if only I didn't talk so much, if only I didn't desire deep conversations and connection with him, if only I were blonde. If I were more of these things, maybe he would love me and show me he cares. I realize there are two people in the relationship. When Josh feels shame, he disconnects, and when I feel disconnected, I feel shame. He hurts me and then I disconnect from him. Then the shame cycle repeats. It's a huge hook in my heart. Before I didn't have a name for it, but now I do."

Let Me tell you what I see. I see your beauty, value, importance, and worth as a wife, mom, sister and friend! I believe you are worth investing in. Condemnation and shame try to steal all the wonderful thoughts I have of you. You are My love and My delight!*

I start to feel something. I feel angry I've lugged this bag around for so long.

"I am drawing a line with this baggage and leaving it here!" I shout. "This has been so painful to carry. I do not want to find my value in another."

I continue to shout, "I want to find it in You. I want to see myself the way You see me! I want to see myself as a beautiful, valuable, important woman, who is worthy of love." I pause and take a big breath. "I want to know You. I want to know Your ways and the width, height, and depths of Your love. I want to know more. I know if I focus on shame and carry it around, I will not fulfill the plans You have for me. I want to live differently. I do not want to live in fear of disconnection."

With excitement and gratitude, I give the snares and hooks of the soul bag to the Baggage Taker.

With delight, I will take the bag. I know shame and condemnation are sources of perpetual frustration in your life. I know it hurts to realize you carried it for so long. Letting go of this bag will cause you to run your race with joy. I am cheering you on! I am not only cheering for you in the stands, but I am running alongside you on this journey. You are not alone, My dear. By believing in Me and My thoughts of you, you will take one of the first steps to make sure you never pick up this bag again. I have something for you to carry in exchange for this bag.

He hands me a rose-gold crown filled with rubies, gold laurel leaves surround the gemstones. The crown design looks familiar; it's from the afghan.

You are royalty, Sandy. You are a daughter of the King. I want you to wear this crown, to remember how I see you, just as you are. This crown has a high value, just like you. With this crown comes authority. You are responsible and have the authority to choose the thoughts which will affect your life.

"Thank you! It is extravagant!" I'm beyond floored receiving such a beautiful thing. I run my fingers over the gemstones and place it on my head.

"I will wear it and remember that I'm Your daughter. You call me Yours, so I belong to You!"

The Baggage Taker sets the green bag aside and looks at the other two bags.

Let's talk about another piece of luggage. Tell Me, what do you see?

I look down at my feet and see the lavender bag. "Eeyore" is stitched on the side. I blurt out, "Really? The depressed donkey from the kids cartoon?"

I start to chuckle and ask myself why I'm carrying this bag. I look inside of the bag and see it's full of dead weeds.

Yes, you are seeing clearly. This depressed donkey has a victim mentality. He has no hope of things getting better. Poor me. This is not who you are. It is no longer poor Sandy, living in hopelessness. I want you to grab hold of daring hope in your marriage, your relationship with Josh and removing the lies you believe about him, your mother's murder case, finding your biological father. You are an overcomer. It's important to mourn and grieve. It's also important to process pain.

My Letters explain it all, you can experience peace when you are courageous to mourn. I want you to acknowledge the loss of your mother, biological father, three sisters, and your childhood house. Give Me everything that hurts. It's important to inventory your thoughts. Who is speaking to you? Is it Me? Is it the Destroyer, or yourself? Not every thought entering your mind is yours or Mine.

If you hold onto pain for too long without inviting Me into your heart to remove it, and to heal the place where the pain lives, a victim mentality will develop and cause decay. Embracing this victim mentality cancels out the power of Me in you. You are not a victim; you are not an orphan. I am with you. You are not alone to figure life out.

It has tormented you with the pain of your mom's death long enough. You have made yourself and your pain an idol. This mentality has become a breeding ground for lies and has paralyzed you from living fully alive. These lies cause defeat, discouragement, and incorrect belief systems to flourish.
Uproot these lies:

> *I am alone.*
> *I am not good enough.*
> *I am not wanted.*
> *Things will never work out for me.*
> *It is the murderer's fault I don't have a good life.*
> *It is my husband's fault I don't have a good life.*
> *I will never know my biological father or ethnicity.*
> *I will never escape this pain. It is hopeless.*

I say you are not alone. You are valuable, wanted, and enough. You are a victor! I have good things in store for you, plans to propel you, not for you to shrivel up and die. I will teach you to recognize and remove lies in your mind and My thoughts will come alive. The Destroyer tries to plant lies. I plant truth and beauty. Remember when you started a cutting garden in your backyard?

"Yes, I wanted to grow flowers for special occasions, and give my fresh cut flowers to my friends. I remember returning from a weeklong trip with my family and found all the flowers I started from seed were dying. The kids and I planted more in the garden. My friend gave me clippings from her garden. As spring arrived, the flowers looked hopeful, as if they would soon produce buds. When my friend Michelle visited me from

Washington D.C., I showed her the garden. We pointed to the same plant. I said it was a flower, she suggested it was a weed. In disbelief I told her it couldn't be possible because I nurtured those plants. I prayed over them, watered them, fertilized them. I wouldn't have taken such great care if I knew they were weeds. Ron, my neighbor, confirmed they were indeed weeds. I remember thinking to myself what a huge waste of time, energy, and money. I was so embarrassed."

The weeds choked your garden like the victim mentality chokes out the donkey's personality. Let's pull these weeds and replace them with beautiful flowers. I will teach you a different way to garden, I will teach you to plant kindness for yourself and help you recognize what should be nurtured and what should get released. I will fill you with compassion. I will teach you to plant mercy, allowing Me to work through you. You will see Me show goodness because I am love. When people challenge you with the snares of offense, condemnation, and shame trying to move you off track, just listen to My words. Love will always win. It never fails.

"I see what you're saying about removing the victim-mentality weeds, they will produce nothing of value or beauty. In the past, it comforted me when people felt sorry for me or reinforced my powerless thoughts. Sometimes I even wanted people to feel sorry for me, it was false comfort." I continue to process these thoughts.

"This victim mentality creates havoc in my life. It has made me refuse responsibility for my own life. I know if I take responsibility, value what You say about me, and believe You have good plans for me, then I will have more confidence in myself. I give You permission to take the weeds. I am uprooting them and throwing them out with the victim mentality baggage!" I exclaim.

Excellent! I will take the bag from you.

We happily look at the work we've accomplished on the green and purple bags.

I have one more piece of baggage I want you to consider removing.

I gaze at its shiny, cherry-red patent leather and its gorgeous gold locks. It looks so expensive. It's so beautiful. I assume its contents are just as expensive and beautiful as its exterior. I think to myself how much I want to keep this bag.

As I open it, my stomach turns with disgust. Immediately I recognize it, but I'm perplexed by the condition.

"How can this be my heart?" I ask the Baggage Taker.

"This is not what I pictured my heart to look like. It's bleeding with holes and black decay spots, gross little worms crawl around it. How could this be my heart? What is going on? How did my heart become this?"

I want to bring you to the moment it happened so you can process this excruciating pain. Sandy, I know this will hurt, but you will reap benefits for the rest of your life if you trust Me.

I hold the Baggage Taker's hand and gently close my eyes. When I open them, I'm with my parents and I look about four years old. My mom's eyes are red from crying as she wipes her nose with tissue.

"Sandy, we want to tell you that something is wrong with Erin. You know how she cries all the time?"

"Yes," I hear in my raspy little voice.

"She is crying because her heart is sick. The doctors will fix her so she will have a good heart."

"If they are fixing her, does that mean her heart is broke?" I ask.

"It does, the doctors will open her heart and fix it. Erin will be in the hospital so they can make her all better."

"Oh, okay."

I run to get my doll, thinking I can give it to her when she's at the hospital.

When you were little, you picked up the tool of denial. You wanted to deny your hurt. You covered this with your smiling face, and with your ignorance of your mother's mental pain and emotional suffering. You have ignored the fact you are carrying around a heart full of pain that's barely functioning. The murder of your mother, the death of your baby sister, losing the twins, the unknown identity of your father, your divorce, the house fire, the drugs and abuse of your childhood have all caused extensive damage to your heart. The cycles of shame in your marriage increase the pain. The snares and hooks cause the holes. Worms of anger circle through the hook's holes of lies. It blocks your ability to receive love and compassion from Me. You can no longer live with this heart.

I remember the first memory of my heart filling with pain when Erin died. She didn't even live seven months. I believe my mother and Roy were so upset and busy, they were consumed with her broken heart and I felt alone. I wonder if I matter to anyone. I'm in my bedroom when my parents get home from the hospital without my sister.

"Sandy, the doctors weren't able to fix Erin's heart. She won't be coming home and we won't see her again." They speak in uniform, trying to hold it together.

I want to reassure them, "Yes, we will see her again."

"No, we won't. She is not with us anymore." I watch my mother leave me completely distraught in my room, offering no comfort or love. Instead she enters her own world of pain.

At the funeral, a little coffin holds a tiny baby body. I peer in and think how sad it is that my sister is in this box.

My mother looks at me and encourages me to touch her. She sweetly brushes Erin's hand. I refuse though, it scares me.

"What will happen to her?" I say with big eyes. "She will go into the ground." Mom whispers.

"Won't it be dark and cold? She won't have anyone with her."

As her big sister, I want to take care of her even when her body is in the ground. I give her my favorite stuffed animal. A sweet freckle-faced black monkey sucking its thumb. I put a little red bandana around the monkey's neck, and I lay it next to my sister.

"You don't have to leave it with Erin," my mom tells me.

I don't want her to be alone, so I keep the stuffed animal there.

The Baggage Taker and I watch as they lower her small casket into the ground. My grown hand is still holding the Baggage Taker's hand as I look at Him, feeling the pain of my four-year-old self.

I know you did not see Me or know Me, but I was with you. I saw you cry, and I cried when you cried. I planned for this healing moment; I knew I would bring you to this place.

I have something for you.

He reaches into his pocket and I notice a glistening box with radiant multi-colored light.

Yes, that is right. I would like to do an exchange because your heart is unsuitable for you. Just as Erin's heart was unrepairable, so is yours. I want to give you a new one. The old heart has been through so much pain, loss, betrayal, and rejection:

> *Losing the identity of your biological father*
> *No closure in your mother's death*
> *Not having a mom*
> *No relationship with your twin sisters*
> *Not having a close family*

I know your deep desire is for family connection. I know you long for family to be there for you and care for you. I know all of this hurts you deeply. I have promises to fulfill your life, but your current heart will only hinder and not help. It is not healthy. With the damage from all the trauma in your life, it is difficult to receive goodness from Me, let alone your friends and family. You were created to receive. You believe the lie that healing is impossible. I want to restore you with a new heart, Sandy!

He hands me the box, and it's sparkling in the sunlight. I slowly open it and immediately feel overwhelmed with love and happiness. I see joy and love. I have wanted this my whole life.

I understand you. This was My original plan for you. My love for you is great and beautiful. With this heart, you will love deeply and it will trigger sensitivity. You will hear My voice, and I will guide you. You will experience emotions besides anger and sadness. Your pain has endured long enough. I created you to experience joy and love. This new heart will function properly and help you live the life I have in store for you. You are My beloved daughter. An intense joy and life will resound from this heart. This is My heart that will reside in you.

I listen deeply. There are no words, just tears. This new heart is a treasure!

"Baggage Taker, thank you for showing me the three bags hindering my journey. I did not understand where the heaviness came from. Now, with a new heart, I feel free! Thank You for showing me the truth of who I am and who You created me to be. I am beautiful like the flowers in my garden. I am no longer a victim. I am a Victor!

Not only did You take the baggage I couldn't carry, but You gave me exactly what I needed, a new heart."

I want you to have one bag for your upcoming trip. When you pack things into this new bag, I want you to remember today and the three bags you gave to Me.

"I accept the new leather bag. It's strong and sturdy, it's the perfect size and color. It's the bag I've been searching for."

Do you see the luggage tag? It has a new name on it, Sandra. I want to call you Sandra because Sandra is who I created from the beginning. Every new adventure you experience, every new challenge you overcome, every new person you meet, you will be Sandra.

I hold the luggage tag and write my address under my new name.

"You have done what I thought was impossible. You have made me whole."

"Baggage Taker, with this heart, I receive all You have for me."

I open my bag and begin packing.

Chapter 12

ADVENTURER

I heard the voice of the Lord saying, "Whom shall I send? And who will go for us?" And I said, "Here am I, send me!"

~ Isaiah 6:8 NKJV

"I'm ready for an adventure! I have a new bag, a new heart, and a new name. I'm ready for a wild ride. Your Letters talk about the "abundant life". I want to experience all You have for me! I do not want to miss out on anything! I want to be Your partner in adventure. I want to explore the world. I love the thrill of excitement and the opportunity for all possibilities to happen. I want to witness an abundant life and allow Your doors to open for me. I trust You to lead the way."

Feeling the spirit of adventure, I begin speaking, "Remember when I could barely drive on the interstate without being anxious? You've brought me so far."

For your first adventure, I want to send you somewhere hidden and off the map. How about an island?

"I've always wanted to visit one. I don't know why, but I'm drawn to the ocean waves and the beach.

The waves are calling me," I reply, laughing and dreaming of the beach.

I have the perfect island in mind, Cuba. I carry this beautiful nation in My heart. The people would say they are forgotten by the world, but it's not true, I've hidden them in My heart. The people have creativity, joy, and contagious love.

"It sounds like the perfect adventure!", I exclaim.

This place holds something I want you to experience. Not only is Cuba a key to the Caribbean, this nation holds a destiny key. It will unlock your purpose.

"I'm excited to go!", I shout out loud. "I want them to know they are not forgotten."

I'm 35 years old and my first experience abroad is to a communist country. As our plane descends, I look out my window to see the beauty of Cuba's palm trees and the variety of unique blues of the ocean below, it looks like a film set from an action movie. The beauty is a nice distraction from my churning stomach. It's my first mission trip with a ministry connected to the Four-Wall Church. It's the ministry team's purpose to bring hope and encouragement to the people of Cuba. I'm nervous, I don't know how we'll get through customs and I've never done this before. I've never traveled internationally.

When the plane lands, the Cuban passengers on the flight clap, delighted by the safe landing. I look around me and I feel like I'm entering a forgotten era, sometime in the 1950s. Beyond the initial tropical beauty, I notice devastation and poverty everywhere. Even from my tiny airplane window, I see half-finished construction projects.

Our ministry team is made up of twelve people. We're from all walks of life. My friend Elizabeth Grace and I are homeschooling moms, there's an army soldier, a sewage waste manager, a doctor and his wife, an intern, a college admissions clerk, a personal assistant, and Marsha, the ministry leader.

As we exit the plane, the team splits up and everyone enters a different customs line. I replay Marsha's suggestions in my mind. Before the trip, she briefed us on language and communicating with customs. The plan is to tell the custom agents we are tourists on vacation. Under any circumstance, we're not to mention we are part of a mission team. I stand in line, I start to second guess myself. What if I say the wrong thing? What if I get interrogated and I accidentally share too much information? What if I get sent home? I certainly don't want to jeopardize the ministry or the Four-Wall Church. I practice my lines in my head. "I'm here for vacation, I'm here for vacation, I'm here for vacation." I mean, I am away from my kids for a week; it's a mommy vacation.

I'm getting closer to the customs agent. I start to look around and notice the people around me. Their dark complexion matches mine. I actually feel like I belong in this airport. I look more like the people here than in Iowa. I feel shame, not looking like my midwestern friends, but here in Cuba, I'm comfortable. I wonder if my biological father is Cuban. I still don't know who he is after all these years. I watch as customs agents dressed in green cotton shirts and dark green pants approach my mission team members, sternly asking all kinds of questions.

I'm next in line. I open my passport, noting the expiration date, 7/17/2022. I begin to approach the counter.

"Why are you in Cuba?" The customs agent asks.

"To see your beautiful beaches," I say with a smile on my face.

The agent is curt with me. She takes my picture, types information into the computer, and lets me pass through the plain paneled room. I exhale and walk towards baggage claim to retrieve my personal bag and one of the team's bags.

Before leaving Iowa, I stuffed ten days-worth of clothes in my new leather carry-on. Usually I overpack for trips, but this time I deprive myself bringing just one tiny bag of toiletries and one blush that multi-tasks as an eyeshadow. I normally fill a carry-on bag just with my hair supplies. This time I remind myself I am on a mission trip. It's not about me and I can forgo the hair supplies. I pick up my bag, find the team's bag, and begin to walk towards the second customs checkpoint.

Do I have anything to claim? No. I walk briskly to the metal detector with my two bags and just as I'm about to the exit, a customs agent stops me. The agent has an intimidating face, her hair pulled back into a tight bun. I look at her name tag, Maria. She points to the mission team's suitcase.

"Do you have a camera in your bag?" she asks in broken English.

"No," I reply matter-of-factly.

It's my understanding there are medical supplies in the suitcase, but I didn't think to check it back in Iowa. Maria ushers me to the side of the room. She tells me to lift the bag on a six-foot stainless-steel table.

"Oh Adventurer, I'm kicking myself, why didn't I look in the luggage? I'm nervous, are You here with me?"

I am, I'm here with you waiting for you to invite Me into the situation, but I'm afraid your own fear is drowning out My voice.

"You're right. Forgive me for not trusting You. I'm new to trusting You. It wasn't my first thought to ask You for help."

I continue to mutter under my breath, "I am so scared. She's asking me if I'm traveling alone. I don't want to get in trouble or sent home."

"Are you traveling alone?", Maria asked repeatedly.

"Uh, yes I am. I'm traveling alone," I lie.

I don't know what to say. We didn't go over it in the briefing. I'm sure it makes little sense to her. Why would an American woman in her thirties who does not speak Spanish fly alone to a communist country? I don't care, I stick to my lie. I take a deep breath and realize I'm on my own.

I'm beginning to feel the familiar sense of abandonment. My palms begin to sweat. The abandonment thoughts roll into anxiety. My need for security and knowing someone has my back is absent in this situation. I know if I jeopardize the team, I'll be sent home and lose the $3,000 I paid to get here. I think about Josh. What would he say? I'd be horrified and wouldn't be able to show my face at church again.

I try to calm down, look around the airport, and begin whispering.

"Adventurer, I see how I let fear run the show. I let fear and anxiety jerk me around."

My perfect love is here for you even though you may not feel it.

"Open the luggage," Maria demands.

I shake my head, trying to snap out of it. Then it hits me, I'm doomed.

Right before we checked the baggage, someone asked me if I wanted to put a padlock on it. I agreed and it never occurred to me I might have to open it for a customs agent. I failed to get the three-number combination when I clicked the lock shut.

I start sweating, "Adventurer! What do I do now?"

I need to get creative. I pretend to look for a key in my floral backpack, knowing I do not have one. After my unsuccessful search, I try using hand signals to communicate, "Sorry, guess we must cut the lock." I cut the air with my fingers simulating scissors. I panic. In my trepidation, I become short with

Maria. She can sense my fear. In a concerned tone, she asks me, "What's wrong?"

I feel convicted.

"Adventurer, is that You? Are You encouraging me to fess up?"

I'm starting to unravel, I can't tell her anything because I'm deep in my own lies. I've created a huge mess involving a piece of luggage that's not even mine.

I scan the airport, praying to see a familiar face, nothing.

"Adventurer, is this part of Your plan for my first international adventure?"

The Cuban customs team now has bolt cutters and are all working on opening the suitcase.

They've added a translator to their team, Carlos.

Carlos is translating my words to the team. He's a handsome man with a warm smile. He unzips the luggage, "What are these items?"

Unfortunately, I discover the contents at the same time as Carlos.

"Oh, Adventurer, help!" I whisper.

Sandra, can you hear Me? Everything is going to be okay.

I nod my head when the luggage flops open to diabetic supplies. I'm relieved, I'm familiar with the items thanks to my diabetic aunt. I kick myself with regret.

"Why, Adventurer, did I lie to Customs and risk getting sent home? Why did the familiar feeling of isolation and loneliness kick in as the team watches from the sidelines?"

Let's talk about this baggage. Let's go a little deeper. Do you see how you have picked up someone else's baggage and have carried it as your own? It seems like you were doing a noble deed, helping the less fortunate, but what was the motive of your heart? On the inside of the baggage was false responsibility. I know the outcome, and I will tell you not to do something when it will not end up being helpful to you or others. It is not always no or always yes. I love it when you listen to My voice and we talk about it. I will lead you. This is your adventure!

"Oh, false responsibility! Why do I fall into this trap?"

You have taken your identity and value from what people think of you, finding value in how they see you. You are more concerned with their thoughts about you than Mine. When we converse, you will see I have the best in store for you. With each situation, you can come for life. You will always have choices set before you. When you listen to My voice, you will know the path of life. My path has peace, joy, and freedom—or the choice that creates condemnation and heartache. This all comes from hearing My voice and journeying on that road.

Carlos pulls out a black plastic box and headpiece from the luggage. I identify this as the source of my trauma.

"What is this?" he asks. Hmmm. What is this? I think to myself. It isn't a camera like the custom team first thought. I start talking slow, looking up into the air, pressing my closed fingertips together trying to communicate in Spanish.

"Do you speak English?" Carlos asks.

"Yes."

"Well, just speak English then!" He demands.

"Oh, yes, of course," I think to myself, "Yes I should just speak English," BUT I'm trying to stall so my brain has more time to answer! I continue with my next thought. I have no idea what this object is, so I make something up.

"It's a receiver for an on-stage moderator," I nod my head up and down. My coat of lies is getting warmer!

Maria comes back, this time angrily speaking Spanish with another customs agent.

"Solo?" I overhear the agent, it's one of the few Spanish

words I know from high school.

"No! No solo!" Maria shouts.

Are my lies exposed? "Oh, Adventurer, does Maria, Carlos, and the entire Cuban customs team know I am deceitful? I feel horrible I'm stuck, but I must dig in my heels there's no turning back now. I can't shift from my original statement, I'm traveling alone to visit Cuba's beautiful beaches."

Oh, Darling, you are not alone. I will never leave you or disown you. This fear of abandonment has tormented you long enough. Do you see how the possibility of being left alone will lead you to deceit? I want you to build trust on this trip, to witness My love for you. I want you to understand what happens when you take on other people's baggage. You have missed the opportunity to trust Me in this situation, but there will be many more in our adventures together.

Carlos sets aside the receiver and headpiece and fills out a yellow form. After he completes it, he asks me to sign.

I stare at the form. It's all in Spanish. I don't understand what I'm signing. This must be it, I must be going home now and I'm signing the form agreeing to my wrongdoing.

Rattled, I ask, "What does it say?"

"It's a form stating we are keeping this receiver. If you want to pick it up, you will need this form back,"

I look at him in shock, "So I can go?"

"Yes."

I sign the form and pick up my belongings. I grip them tight, shell-shocked from the whole ordeal, and stiffly walk over to the currency exchange counter.

"Oh, Adventurer! I get to stay in Cuba with my team! I have a second chance to continue the adventure!"

I assume customs continues to watch me as I walk away, so keeping with my story, I pretend I'm alone and get $100 of currency exchanged. I walk out of the airport and immediately feel I'm on the red carpet. As I walk outside into the heat, I notice many people lining the old metal gates, waiting for their loved ones to arrive. Dazed and traumatized I walk the concrete pathway until my team leader spots me.

"I'm so sorry," she says.

She tries to hug me, but in my most urgent voice I whisper in her ear.

"Don't hug me. I told them I was alone. They might still be watching me."

"It's okay," she says. "Our Cuban leader spoke to the customs agents. They know we're all together."

My heart sinks. Are you kidding me? All of that for nothing? How embarrassing! The bus pulls to the curb and we load our bags and get onboard. I sink in my seat, I'm exhausted but paranoia settles in.

"Oh Adventurer, what if they are following me?"

If they are, do you trust Me? Do you believe I can take care of you?

"Yes, I trust You!"

We arrive at the Cuban Four-Wall Church where the first group is already waiting for us at the outdoor patio area. The second half of the team walks over to the patio. Everyone seems worried, wondering what happened. They assure me they were praying for me. Someone laughs and gives me the padlock code. I wouldn't need it anymore since the lock was out. The code was 316, for John 3:16. Of course it was. I pull my friend Elizabeth aside. She's been to Cuba many times and invited me on this trip.

"Is the Cuban government following me?" I ask.

"No dear, you're okay," she assures me.

Relief fills me. But I still wonder what form I signed. Checking with the Cuban leader, he assures me the paper is as

Carlos described.

"Oh, Adventurer, it encourages me to know everyone was praying for me, but I didn't feel anything. I was consumed by my own fear and paranoia, I couldn't feel or hear anything else."

I begin to think about my past, the familiar feeling of loneliness. I felt the same gripping fear of the unknown when my mom came home drunk and with bated breath. I waited wondering if she would start a fight or leave me alone in my bed. I felt the fear of bad news. Fear came with Erin's death, my mom's death, and the house fire. It's the same fear of getting in a fight with Josh and wondering if he will leave me. My fear-filled thoughts cripple me.

Sandra, I didn't give you a spirit of fear. I gave you a sound mind. Know I am always at work, even when you are unaware of what I am doing. I love to work through My children. If you travel with Me, you'll discover My adventures will always end in My kindness and goodness. Know I am with you, and you don't have to agree with fear.

"Oh, Adventurer, why did I have to go through all of that?"

Training. It's as simple as that.

"Training? What kind of training is that?"

Training to think differently. You will be transformed when you renew your mind. You will learn to do things differently in your life. I will give you experiences that will accelerate the rewiring of your thinking. You have experienced a lot of fear, abandonment, and trauma in your life. I will give you new experiences so you will trust Me. This battle is in your head. I will speak to your heart and help shift the thoughts in your head. You will listen to My voice over the Destroyer's lies. It's a process of learning to enjoy the journey. We are in this adventure of life together! Some of the adventurers will be challenging and others will be revealing or surprising, but each one will unfold My heart of love for you.

I close my eyes and begin to feel the transformation deep within my new heart.

Our first event on the mission trip is a celebration night for the community. Before the event starts, we sit in plastic chairs in a church member's house to discuss details of the event. It's a clean old house with lively bright colored walls. I take my seat in a plastic chair and notice Robert passing by me, he is an 86-year-old dentist.

That will be Kingston, long after you are gone, he will be an old missionary, just like Robert.

Tears burst from my eyes, "Really?"

Yes, I put a heart in him to travel and take my good news of love to the nations. Just like you named him, Kingston Justus, he will bring justice to the world.

Robert walks by again. Tears overtake me again as I remember the Adventurer's words.

As a team, we plan for the evening's party. Together we go over logistics and details and everyone is assigned a role for the event.

Hours later, we gather in the same room and push the plastic chairs up against the wall, transforming the room. Instantly, it becomes a dance floor, and our team begins to worship.

"Now this is praise and worship!" I yell to Renee, also known as the dancing doctor.

In the moment, I can feel the spirit of joyful dancing from the Other Side, it's an indescribable sensation. I feel elevated, every worry washes right off my back. I've never experienced worship like this before. Everyone is dancing, laughing, smiling, clapping, and singing. I even break my flip flop while I'm dancing. My heart is so full, I feel freedom, I'm a different person on this island. I've become the person I was supposed to be all along. I'm free from fear and insecurity, radiating light and love.

When the night ends, I hobble onto the bus with my broken flip flop. I find my seat and Tom, the waste management employee from Wisconsin, sits next to me on the bus.

"Fun dancing! I bet your kids think you're a fun mom!" He exclaims.

I laugh. His words resonate with me. He's right, I have the potential to be the fun mom. I think about my kids at home, wondering what they're up to. They deserve a fun, engaged mom, not the angry one I've been for years.

The next morning, we prepare ourselves for street evangelism. As an American, I cannot proselytize in Cuba. If I'm caught, I'll be thrown in jail. So, our collective group of Cubans and Americans team up. The Americans silently pray while the Cubans talk to people about the invitation extended by the Adventurer, to know Him in a personal way.

We meet with several people, interested and accepting our message. Before we walk away, we encounter a blind man named Sergio. He is well known on the island for sharing the heart of the Adventurer with people.

"Adventurer, I want to know if someone can share Your heart with me better than I can hear You for myself."

I have something I want to say through Sergio. Even though he doesn't see with his natural eyes, he can see with his spiritual eyes.

"I want to hear what You would say to me."

I gather my courage to ask Sergio if there is anything he can share, any insight from the heart of the Adventurer.

He becomes still, then Sergio speaks from the heart of the Adventurer,

Whatever you touch, it will be made new. Whatever you want to do, you are going to do it because I am with you. Today I activate a new gift that you have been waiting for and asking for a long time. Today, I activate it in you.

My knees hit the floor because this is true. I want to experience the love of the Adventurer in a tangible way.

You have new armor. You are going to shine like silver, and there is going to be a new joy in your life. Because you are My daughter. You are My daughter! There is a fountain that comes out from the depths of Earth, a new water, and you are standing in front of that fountain. The water flows and falls on your body. Your clothing is changing and taking the majesty of God. Today you will see what you have been asking for a long time. There is a jewel case. The key of that case is not in your hands, it's in your mouth, the key to the treasure chest is in your mouth.

Sergio smiles.

I touch my hands to my lips and begin to laugh. I laugh so hard I can't stand, I fall to my knees. I am surrounded by love and laughter on the floor. I try to stand, and I'm completely overtaken with joy. I have wanted to experience the Adventurer's heart of love for a long time and here it is showing up in laughter.

"Adventurer, what did you mean about my clothing

changing?"

Clothing is a metaphor for identity. I want you to see yourself as I see you.

"In Your Letters You say, 'As I am in this world, so are you.' Is that what You mean?"

Yes, I want you to reflect Me as you shine like silver. You have a redemptive story. I want you to share your story. Blessings come out of the jewel case when you speak. This is not only for you but for those who hear.

You are a daughter of purpose. You were destined to be My daughter. Before the foundations of the world, I chose you. I know you don't know your biological father, but I want you to know Me. You are My daughter, I brought you to Cuba for you to experience how I take care of My kids. I'm with you the entire way and I will never leave you. You are one of My children. No matter the lies, the danger, the uncertainty, I have a purpose for you, and I want you to move into the plans I have for you. But you must know in your heart, you are My daughter first before you minister to anyone. This is key. I know you came to Cuba to minister to others, but I want you to allow Me to minister to you first, and from that place you can encourage others with the words I encourage you.

"Oh Adventurer, Thank You for allowing me to experience Your extravagant love in a tangible way. I want to go on more adventures with You!"

Going off the map and under the radar will be your normal one day. This is the beginning of international adventures! And your question is answered.

"What question?" I ask Him.

At Erin's grave you wondered if you were a daughter of purpose like your sister Erin. Now you know. You are My daughter of purpose and I will bring meaning and redemption to the places of your heart. It will be a wild adventurous ride.

Chapter 13

Territory Taker

For the weapons of our warfare are not carnal but mighty in God for pulling down strongholds...

~ 2 Corinthians 10:4 KJV

Lying in my dark bedroom, I toss and turn. It's been almost twenty years since my mom's murder and I still wonder if it will ever be solved. We haven't had an arrest. I want resolution, I want to let this go and move on.

I can't sleep, so I decide to go downstairs to the kitchen for a tall glass of water. I flick the kitchen light on and see Karis' homework sprawled on the dining table. There is scattered paper everywhere; a notebook, pencils, pens, a highlighter, and a history textbook open to the chapter on the Mexican American War. As I tidy her mess, I read from her textbook, "Manifest Destiny, the idea that the United States is destined by God to expand and spread democracy across the North American Continent." Karis scribbled in the margin, "to take territory". I sit down at the dining table and begin to read her history notes. I see movement from the corner of my eye and look up. At first I'm startled, but then relieved to see another Facet is taking a seat next to me.

"Hello!"

Hello Sandra. What are you reading?

I look down at her history notes.

"I'm trying to understand the concept of taking territory. I can't sleep. My mother's murder continues to haunt me. I grieve the lack of an arrest and I just can't let it all go."

Sandra, I want you release the resolution of your mom's death to Me. Holding on is hurting your heart. I want to give you weapons, strategies, and tools to keep this new heart healthy. The land of your heart is the territory we want to occupy. The Destroyer tries to find access into your heart. He is sly and sends his pests to wreak havoc but remember he is not creative. He uses the same wiles and schemes from long ago. He tells the same lies. He tries the same tricks. How often do you hear a married person who wants a divorce say, 'I never really loved him or her.'

That is the Destroyer's tactic to slip a lie into the heart. He will even come in as your voice in a thought, until you believe it's your voice. He's always offering a counterfeit offer. In My Letters, I put it in Nehemiah's heart to rebuild the walls of Jerusalem. Jerusalem is the heart, or home, for the Jews. I want you to look at Jerusalem as a picture of your heart. Remember when you were desperate for Me to heal your heart?

"Yes, I didn't think it was possible. I was at a loss of what to do."

You're right it is impossible to do on your own. Nehemiah's mission was impossible, too, but just like I put it in Nehemiah's heart to rebuild, I put it in yours. I want to occupy the place of your whole heart. It's important to be aware if you have given a part of your heart over to someone or something else. I want to equip you to keep your heart in My hands.

"I never want to pick up the heart baggage I once carried."

You won't when you put the right walls around your heart. In Nehemiah's days the wall around Jerusalem was destroyed. The walls were over 8ft thick and 40ft high with several watchtowers and gates. It's important to have walls to protect and strengthen our bond and keep good thoughts in, and recognize the counterfeit walls erected by offense, hurt, pain, and disappointments. As you know, these must be shaken.

The Territory Taker lays out a map of my heart. There's a beach, garden, waterfalls, and a blanket of stars in a dark night sky. On the map I notice broken places, too. I see construction sites and mounds of rubble. My eye immediately is drawn to the areas in need of work instead of the beauty on the map.

You are altogether beautiful My love, there is no flaw in you. Don't worry about those areas. In due time, we will take care of them. In Nehemiah's days, the people were willing to work to rebuild the walls and join Nehemiah on the mission. I knew how desperate you were to receive a new heart. This is precious to Me. Desperation draws Me in. The Jews set to work with a tool in one hand and held a weapon in the other. Are you ready to see the tools and weapons I have prepared for you? Let's go back to this spot.

He points to the Glory Beach on the map. I close my eyes and glory flecks wash over me and I'm transported to the beach. I look down and see a rope tied around my ankle. My eyes follow the rope, looking for the other end, and notice it's in the ocean. I'm limited, I can only move so far.

"Can you get this off? What am I tied to?"

You are stuck. You are anchored to your mother's murder. Remember when I asked you before if you were ready to let this go? You told Me you were ready, but your heart wasn't ready.

I tug on the rope, realizing it won't release. "It's true! I can't do it! I feel if I let this go then it means my mother's death will be forgotten, that it won't matter anymore. Why do You want this?"

You've allowed this to take over your heart. It has consumed you and limited you. This is not what I want for your life or for your future. I have a weapon for you called 'Letting Go'. When you let go, it is a position of the heart. In the war for heart ground, it allows Me to occupy. Letting go allows Me to move on your behalf. This weapon annihilates the tactics of the Enemy to keep you stuck.

"When you ask me to use the 'Letting Go' weapon, I feel you are asking me to let go of my mother, too."

That is not true. You have wrapped up your mother's identity and her death as one. It's difficult for you to separate them. Dwelling on the murder and worrying how it will be solved has taken over your identity. If you want to move forward, the first step is to sever the rope with this weapon.

I take the weapon and I slash the rope, in faith. I know it will move my mind closer to experiencing freedom.

"But I want someone held accountable for what they did."

I know. I want to talk about what this is doing to you and bring you closure. I want you to go back to Bill's retirement party. Remember when you traveled to eastern Iowa to celebrate his retirement?

"Yes, I remember."

I'm going to take you there. After you grab your cake and punch, walk over to the two ladies sitting at the large circular table in the ballroom. Sit with them. I want you to meet some of the other guests you didn't meet that day.

"Okay, I'll do as You suggest."

Immediately I'm transported to a hotel ballroom, surrounded by people I don't recognize, all dressed up for the occasion. I get a slice of cake and glass of punch and begin walking over to the two ladies sitting alone at a round table.

"Hello ladies, may I sit here?"

"Sure, go right ahead."

"Thanks." I put my cup and plate down on the table and scoot the chair out.

"Do you both live here in the area?"

"No, we live close, how about you?"

I take my seat and drink from my glass. "I'm from eastern Iowa but I now live in central Iowa," I reply. "How do you know Bill?"

While the older woman talks, the younger one excuses herself to get more punch.

"That's my daughter, Janice. We don't talk about my other daughter, Lori or her death. We met Bill when he worked the homicide case for my daughter."

"Oh, I'm sorry to hear of your loss. Did they arrest the person who killed her?"

"Oh yes, it was my son-in-law. He's in jail now. Bill was the Special Agent that worked the case and he cared about our situation."

"Oh, that's so terrible. I'm so sorry."

My heart hurts realizing murder is our common ground. I'm broken to learn another person's horrific story. The thought of another hate-filled murder sinks in, it's heart shattering to think about one human killing another.

"How do you know Bill?" Louise wonders.

"He worked my mother's murder case," I'm saddened by my own words.

"I'm sorry. How awful not to have your mother in your life. My son-in-law apologized for killing her. I take care of my grandkids now. My daughter Janice and I pretended like nothing happened and moved on."

I cringe inside. How could they not talk about someone

they love? Not talking about her seems like she never existed. And have they really moved on or are they stuck like me? An immense sadness overcomes me, as my heart breaks for their family.

When Louise finishes, Janice returns to our table, sits down, and finishes her punch. Bill comes over to our table and introduces us to his wife and son.

In the seventeen years of knowing Bill, I've never met his wife or family. I shake their hands.

"I appreciate your husband and what he did for my mother's case."

They smile and his wife proudly rubs Bill's back. He looks around the room trying to find people he can introduce me to. He finds a few of his friends and colleagues.

"This is Sandra, I worked her mother's case. I wasn't able to bring her closure," he says with a sad tone in his voice.

My mother's case is one of the few he didn't solve. Every year that passes makes it much harder to solve. I look at him, and his friend offers a slight smile trying to reassure him.

"It's okay, Bill."

When "It's okay" leaves my mouth, I think to myself, "Is it really okay"? He nods, thanks me for coming, and continues to move around the room.

As I finish my cake, Bill's colleague invites anyone to come to the stage and share a memory of Bill.

Emotion takes over as I make my way to the microphone in the hotel's ballroom. I start crying as I walk to the podium, feeling sentimental, thankful for his work, and afraid his retirement symbolizes a closed door on my mother's case. I reassure him it's okay he didn't solve her case.

No one spent more time on her case than Bill. Maybe we all took on too much false responsibility. I'm ready to release him from that.

Looking at Bill's loved ones I begin to speak.

"I met Bill on one of the worst days of my life. That day, my family learned my mother's death was not an accident, but a cover-up of her brutal murder. After years of facing the unimaginable, he was always thorough and warm to my family. He was always encouraging and understanding. Sometimes the hero doesn't look like capturing the bad guy, it looks like helping and investing in one person. For me, it looked like coming alongside my family and me in the most violent, painful situation of our lives and listening. Bill is my hero. He always made time for me and answered the questions he could. He had compassion and cared for my mother's case and for me. I'm thankful for the time Bill and Detective Scheetz put into my mother's case."

Looking at Bill, I add, "It will never be wasted. I appreciate all that you have done for my family. Thank you."

Instead of finding my seat, I collect my things and leave the room. Not sure where else to go, I start walking to my car.

"Territory Taker, is it really okay? Is it okay he couldn't solve her case?"

It is okay to stop worrying about the ending. It is okay to stop trying to figure it all out. It is okay to move on with your life.

"I feel it when You say it. There is a freedom to using the 'Letting Go' weapon in this moment. You know I still love her. It's okay for me to move on from her death and have a great life."

It's okay.

Then I whisper, "I'm letting go of this."

Supernatural peace floods my car. I see myself closing the chapter, shutting the book, and burying it. I no longer need to keep mulling over my mother's death. Nothing good has come of it, only the heaviness of my heart and my mind. I close my eyes and see myself on Glory Beach again.

"Your love and truth have shed light on my heart. I feel lighter now. I'm not weighed down in my thoughts. I feel so good right now. I'm free! Thank You Territory Taker for this powerful weapon!"

I'm so proud of you! You can overcome hard things. With My hand in yours we can take great territory! Are you ready to gain more ground? I want to expand your heartland, let's go to Mexico again. This time, let's take your kids!

In excitement, I give the cheerleading rally cry to my kids.

"Are you guys ready? We are leaving for our first adventure together! Tijuana, Mexico here we come!"

Looking out the window of the plane, I hear the Territory Taker's whisper.

Look how far you've come. Now, here you are traveling on another mission; this time in Mexico with your own children. You adventurer, you! I'm so proud of you! There is a reward that occurs from tuning into My voice. When you honor Me by listening, I've got something wonderful in store.

Remember, the dream I gave you about the majestic wave? First, you were driving a white SUV on a bridge. Your entire family was in the car. You told your family to peer out the window to the ocean. Looking from a bird's-eye view you said, 'Look at that wave!' There was an enormous, majestic wave. A glass wall divided the wave allowing you to peer into the wave from a distance.

"Yes, I remember!"

In my mind's eye I see the end of a road. It seems I'm trying to drive down a river, then I see my old neighbor Marian. As I struggle to steer, I think to myself, "Where do I go?" I roll up the window. The water is now in the vehicle, but the river is overtaking the car and I have no control. Suddenly, a huge wave is in front of us. We are moving down the waterfall and JJ, my oldest, grasps for my hand in worry. I take his hand and reassure him it will be okay.

Mexico is the beginning of the night dream I showed you three years ago. The wave symbolizes the Youth With A Mission wave. A river, a flood, a wave, a waterfall, my spirit will overtake your family! It all started with a yes! I'm going to move hearts in your family.

Here we are overlooking the ocean. I'm in awe by its vastness and beauty. I'm also in awe I made it to Tijuana, Mexico with my kids all by myself. The last time I was in Mexico, some missionaries recommended I return with my kids. I thought it was the best idea ever.

"Territory Taker, I want them to see how other people in this world live. I want them to have a heart for other cultures and people. My kids are 14, 12, and 10. This is one of my dreams, doing mission work with my kids. However, I need help. The kids are missing home because they want their friends and video games. They are fighting amongst themselves, whining and complaining, begging for their phones. I want them to live life with people, not in front of a screen. I know I'm brave, not for bringing them down here but for taking their phones away and expecting them to be present."

You are brave! Territory is being taken in their hearts, you just don't see it yet.

I'm not getting any sleep. I'm waking up four times a night, wide awake. I'm in over my head this time. What seemed like a great idea, teaching my kids to be selfless, turns out to be really hard work. I love traveling to other nations and I thought they would too. When I envisioned us coming to Mexico, connecting as a family, and meeting people from all over the world, I thought it would be wonderful. But, it's a fight just to keep them from whining. I feel I have failed as a mother. I don't think I'm taking ground, I'm losing it. I want to quit.

I even check to see how many miles it is to drive home. I think renting a car and getting out of here would be a great idea. JJ found his phone and snuck off with it. Kingston threw a body rolling tantrum on the bed. The kids keep asking when we're done after an hour of volunteering. I feel I have no authority as a parent. The kids won't listen when I tell them to stop. I can tell JJ is resenting me, forcing him to come with his siblings. I'm frustrated with my volunteer coordinator who is in her early twenties and is disorganized. I want to keep my kids busy and coming all this way for a couple of hours of landscaping in the morning is frustrating.

"I feel alone. I wonder if I missed Your purpose. If this is Your will, then why am I drowning?"

Look at Me. You're not drowning. I'm teaching you how to ride the wave. Take My hand. You think you're in over your head and it is overwhelming. Really, it is the best place to be. You can't trust yourself, or your abilities, or your surroundings. We are going deeper in trust! You will need to solely rely on Me in the new territory. When you trust Me, My peace encompasses your heart, and it will take you deeper into a place of trust and stillness. Let peace arise. The deeper you swim in the water, the more freedom you'll feel around you. Give Me your trust and My peace can guide you through this.

Remember, you aren't alone! Remember, I am with you, always! I work through people. I work through your hands. As My warrior, I give you authority. Take every thought captive. You are responsible for your thoughts. So many people want help but reading My Letters and hearing My voice to declare over the lies will change how you think. My words tell you that you are not alone, but you don't believe them.

"Territory Taker help my unbelief! Help me be brave!"

If you step out, I will provide the grace. You heard Me in your dream, calling out for you to visit Mexico with your kids. Just as you love and delight when your kids listen without whining and complaining, I do too! I make a provision of grace. It may not look like what you thought. However, I provide grace when you listen to My call.

It is critical to ask, 'Territory Taker, what are you doing?'

Here, take these glasses, they are a tool. A tool to see My perspective in troublesome situations. Let Me show you, put them on and ask a question.

"So, what are You doing with my kids?"

I slide the glasses on, and I see clearly what the Territory Taker is doing.

I'm planting seeds in the land of your kids' hearts. I'm establishing something in them that will affect generations. I'm softening their hearts to have compassion for others. I'm bringing out gifts I've placed in them. See what I'm doing with JJ. He stepped out of his comfort zone and gave an encouraging word to a teenager he didn't know at the youth meeting. He shared My heart with a Korean boy. JJ will go to the nations! Expanding heart territory isn't a comfortable thing. It's about exposing lies, kicking them out and replacing them with truth. What have you been doing each morning here in Mexico?

"Landscaping," I say with frustration.

Specifically, you have been pulling weeds. Baby ones are hard to grasp with big fingers. But a medium sized one is easier to detect. Sometimes if they get too big, you don't know if they are a part of the landscaping.

"How about aerating the soil?"

Yes, turning the soil over. Exposing what's underneath and bringing it to the light. It's cleansing. Take heart My warrior, the territory is wide for the taking. Release My words into the land. Release what I'm saying over yourself, kids, and the land.

I look down at my feet, shuffling them in the dirt.

"Thank you, I'm a territory taker, just like You!"

I have one more weapon I want you to discover:

The Weapon of Forgiveness. This is powerful. My authority is released into a situation when you forgive. You have done this before, but you may not have seen in the light what I'm about to show you. When you forgive, it removes all entry points blocking the Destroyer's access to your heart. It's like when the Jews left a hole in the wall they were restoring. The Destroyer will leave a hook to pull your emotions around. However, when you forgive, he will have nothing to use against you or come into your heart. Do you need to forgive?

Faces of people flood my mind. They're all familiar faces I need to forgive.

Forgiveness allows for a divine exchange. I will take the offense and exchange it for something supernatural. If you forgive the murderer, your heart will expand.

"I'm not ready for that. I don't think I could ever do that!"

When you are ready, forgiveness will unlock things you didn't have access to before. I give peace, healing, and you can hear Me better. When you hold onto the bitterness, anger, and victimization in your heart it will only lead to torment.

"I don't want to live with those in my heart, but I think I need some more time. Is there anyone else You want me to forgive?"

Yes, what about Jim?

I pause and take a deep breath, "Oh boy, I'm not sure. He was so awful to me when I was little. His abuse has haunted me for thirty years."

I set the forgiveness standard. I have forgiven you for your sins, even sins you have intentionally done. There were situations where you needed to act and you didn't. I forgive you for those too. The times you have held hate in your heart, I forgive you, therefore I ask you to forgive others. Jim needs your forgiveness, Sandra.

Chapter 14

HEALER

Then they cried to the Lord in their trouble, and he saved them from their distress. He sent out his word and healed them; he rescued them from the grave.

~ *Psalm 107:19, 20 KJV*

My cell phone rings, its Sarah, one of my mom's friends. I'm in the middle of a project, but I answer it anyway. I haven't heard from her in years.

"Hello?"

"Sandra, it's Sarah. I know it's been a long time. Jim (another family friend) had a stroke and he's in the ICU. His wife Anne, asked me to call you. If you're available, could you visit him? The doctors don't think he is going to make it, he's in a coma. His family will be taking him off life support."

I'm shocked.

"Oh, my goodness. I appreciate you letting me know. I can visit later this afternoon."

"That would be great. I know Anne would appreciate seeing you… The ICU is on the second floor, he's in room…"

Her voice trails off as I begin to imagine Jim in the ICU.

This has caught me off guard. Sarah's voice fades into the background as I try to comprehend why Anne would want me there. I'm sad to hear about his stroke, but I haven't heard from them in years. We haven't really talked since my mother's death. I start thinking how I'll re-arrange my afternoon schedule to visit the hospital.

"Sandra? Are you there, did you get all of that?"

"Yes, I'm here. I will visit later today. Thanks for the call, I appreciate you reaching out."

"Thanks for being willing to visit him. I think it will mean a lot to them. I will see you there."

I hang up the phone, grab my keys and head out the door. I start my car and text Josh.

> Me: Hey, one of my mom's friends, Jim, had a stroke. I'm going to the hospital, I feel compelled to visit him. Not sure how long it will take, can you please pick up the kids after school? I'll get dinner on my way home.
>
> Josh: Okay Honey. I will be praying. Drive Safe.

I shift the car in reverse and back out of the driveway, pausing in the middle of the road, contemplating what direction I should begin driving. The hospital is only 20 minutes away, but I need to process my thoughts and just drive. I look in my rearview mirror.

Sandra, is it okay if I ride along with you?

"Sure, I don't know where I'm heading, but I could use some company." I look deep into the Healer's eyes.

My thoughts are disruptive and scattered. I pass Kingston's elementary school and I think back to the moment I saw an eight-year-old girl in Tijuana's Red-Light District. The first thing I noticed was a big hickey on her neck. What hope does a young girl have in such a broken place?

As I continue driving, I look back in the mirror again.

"Healer, do You truly heal? Do You heal the deepest, most intimate wounds? Do You heal the broken-hearted? Do You heal emotional pain from sexual trauma?"

I have made provision for healing hearts, minds, and bodies. I will not only heal your heart, but I can use it to impact the person who initiated the pain. I reveal how to forgive.

"Will You help me? I have hidden a secret for too long."

In order to go forward, we need to go back. Are you ready for that?

My car slows to a red light and I turn around and look at the Healer in the backseat.

"Where do we need to go?"

We need to go back to the time your innocence was taken, and your voice was lost.

The light changes to green, I slowly press the gas pedal.

"I know the memory You are thinking of. It makes me sick to my stomach. I try never to think about it. Why do we have to go back to that moment? Can't You release heavenly love and healing over me?"

Mending is a process. Healing from a trauma takes courage and bravery. I want you to know that I'm with you the whole time and you won't have to walk through this by yourself. You are not alone. I want you to understand I want restoration for you. Let's go to the memory of that night. I will let you go there when you are ready. When you are ready, you can share.

I see a nearby park and decide I need to stop driving to process the memory. I pull into a parking spot, turn off the engine and roll down my window. I watch kindergartners playing on the swing set, chasing one another around the play structure. I look back at the Healer again.

"Alright. I trust You, I'm ready to talk about that night."

I'm eight-years-old when my parents host a big weekend party at our old house on Black Diamond Trail. I remember seeing my dad's bandmates from Foolish Pleasure lounging around drinking from brown bottles with red and white labels. Loud music blares from a tower of speakers. A thick cloud of smoke hangs low in the living room. Couples sprawled out on our couches, making out, oblivious to others around them.

I feel relieved to see familiar faces at the party. My parent's friends are all here. I'm overwhelmed with so many people in the house.

As the party rages on, more strangers stumble into the house and my parents are getting drunk. I'm scared and seek refuge in their bedroom. I close the door behind me, turn off the lights, and hide under the covers, praying no one comes in their room and discovers me. The music downstairs is thumping, people are screaming. I'm wide awake, gripping the covers, hoping I grow tired and eventually fall asleep like my brother had hours ago.

Eventually I hear the door slowly open, so I shut my eyes and try to relax my body, pretending to be asleep. The person slowly approaches the bed trying to walk quietly but is clearly drunk and stumbling to the bed. I can smell his sour body odor and the smoky, alcohol stench lingering on his breath. It's a familiar smell, I recognize it's Jim. He throws off the covers and scoops his arms under my limp body. I pretend to stay asleep, disturbed by his smell as he carries me out of my parent's room and into my bedroom. His rough hands slowly crawl beneath the waistband of my pants. He molests me. I don't stop him. I just lay there, trying to understand what Jim is doing to me. He closes the door and leaves me alone on my bed.

"Healer, were You there the night, in my room, watching as

this happened to me? Why didn't You stop it?"

Healer doesn't respond. He wants me to continue telling my story.

I sit up on my bed, I clench my arms around my legs and start rocking myself. I'm scared. I start to cry, "Why did this have to happen to me?" I suck my thumb. I don't know what to do.

"Were You with me when I tried to comfort myself?"

Healer continues to listen, offering no words of insight.

I wait until the music gets softer and guests shout their goodbyes from the front yard. I know the party is winding down, so I muster the courage to find my mom.

People are passed out on the floor, some in the kitchen. I eventually find her laughing with some friends and interrupt her.

"Can you come talk to me on the porch?"

I don't know how to tell her what Jim did to me. I feel so dirty and gross. Will she listen to what I have to say?

As soon as we get to the porch, I blurt it out, "Jim carried me to my room and put his hands down my pants," I utter.

She slurs her speech.

"He did what to you?"

She keeps repeating the phrase. Her voice is getting louder with each completion of the question. It seems her slow comprehension of the situation increases each time she repeats it.

She brings me into the mod kitchen with white, gold, and avocado colored wallpaper. She sits me on the metal trim table. She pushes in hard on my ears. Immediately I feel shame and my voice is gone. She tells my dad and others around what happened.

"Can I stop there, Healer? It is so humiliating. He is a family friend. I trusted my mom to keep it to herself. Instead she drunkenly marches off and tells everyone. I see the direct action of my words creating chaos and consequences around me. I made a mess, and I feel like it is my fault."

I hear her yell words from the second story of the old house, I don't understand how words immediately clothe me in embarrassment.

"Get out of my house you're a child molester!" She screams.

I'm so uncomfortable. The music stops, and the party comes to a scathing halt as I sit on the couch by myself. I watch as Jim and Anne bustle out of the house. I don't remember anything else that night.

I want you to pause and look at Me. There is no reason to look down My dear. I want to share with you what and where I am. Ask Me again, ask Me where I am in that memory.

"Yes, where were You? Didn't You care?"

Then I see in my mind's eye Healer carrying me up the steps to my room. I'm holding onto His neck like a koala bear clinging to a eucalyptus tree. Tears fall from my burning eyes.

What do you need at that moment?

"I want to be held and supported. You are holding me and comforting me now. That is what I need, and I don't get it from my parents. I don't need a humiliating and embarrassing scene. I need the care and comfort of my mother. I need a protective father. I need to know it is not my fault he violated me. I later feel betrayed by some of my family for continuing a relationship him.

I want you to do something that may seem offensive to you.

"Oh great, what is it? What if I don't want to?"

It is a choice; you do not have to do this.

"Okay... What do you want me to do?"

I want you to forgive him.

"You want me to do what!? That's impossible. You were

there. You saw what he did. I was only eight years old!"

Forgiving is about you not living in torment and having tortured thoughts. This is not saying that what he did to you is okay. It is horrific what he did! This releases you from being emotionally tangled up with his actions. An unforgiving heart opens you to lies and deceit about yourself and ultimately who I made you to be. You are a reconciler and an ambassador of My healing love. How can you be who I want you to be when you have taken on these false identities as though they were truth?

I am stunned, unable to comprehend all of this at one time. I don't think I even know how to forgive.

I have a gift for you if you chose to accept it. It is the gift of compassion. Compassion gives you an eye to see how I see. Compassion is the key to forgiveness. It cannot be manufactured. It is not a formula. True compassion shifts hearts and can only come from My heart. I want to give you a glimpse of Jim's life as a boy.

It moved me.

The Healer's heart for Jim helps me see this person differently, as a person the Healer desires to make a difference in his life.

In your lifetime, you will endure many challenging moments, but I have plans to reach hearts because of your forgiveness. Remember, forgiveness is a powerful weapon. Forgiveness is progressive and it starts a chain reaction. You won't be in this place of torment with him. When you forgive, you are no longer connected to him. Those things he's done to you go back to him and you no longer carry them.

Because I love and My love heals, it covers a multitude of wrongs if people will receive it. My love can sometimes offend. People want to justify why hearts hold onto anger. It only numbs the heart. I offer so much to My people, but pride will keep them from receiving or allowing Me to do significant work in their hearts. I have forgiven you and your short-comings, and you are My child.

I want you to let go of this heartache that is tethering your heart. Healing will come. Are you ready?

"I think so. You were for me, with me, and by my side that night. Thank You, I can learn to forgive."

Forgive all the things that come to your mind.

I forgive Jim for molesting me.
I forgive my mother for being drunk and handling it so poorly.
I forgive my dad for not protecting me as I thought he should.
I forgive myself for not yelling and getting away.
I forgive.

In this powerful moment, a scrubbing is taking place. The Healer instantly removes the shame, guilt, condemnation, and silence with healing waves. Glory washes over my heart and deep in my soul. I feel lighter. I feel the heaviness leave my body.

Are you ready to keep driving and go to the hospital now?

I take another deep breath.

"Yes, I think so."

I start my car up again and type the hospital address into my phone map app. As I press the gas pedal, I immediately feel dread. Today is Jim's last day on Earth. I feel sick with the thought he's dying today, and he doesn't know the power of the Healer. I look back again in the rearview mirror. "Healer, what is going on with Jim?"

A spirit of death is encapsulating Jim. Pray with the authority I have given you to break off the spirit of death.

So, I pray, "Healer, remove a spirit of death encapsulating Jim."

As I pull into the hospital's parking ramp and walk into the skywalk, my phone rings, it's Sarah.

"Where are you?"

"I'm walking into the hospital now."

"You aren't going to believe this!"

"Try me."

"Jim woke up and he is responding. He's going to live!"

"Wow! That was a powerful prayer," I say.

I know this is the Healer's work. Since forgiving him, I'm not afraid to talk to him. Sarah meets me in the skywalk and shares more news of his transformation. As I listen to Sarah, I have the urge to talk to Anne and I want to pray for Jim.

Ask Anne for permission to pray for her husband.

Anne comes up to me and I give her a tight squeeze.

"Thank you for coming," she whispers in my ear.

"Anne, I want to pray for Jim, would you mind?"

"You know I believe in reincarnation."

"I know you do, I want to tell him about the Healer."

"Sure, you can go in."

We walk into the sterile hospital room and I see Jim, helpless, tubes connect to his nose and other tubes hook up to beeping machines. The slow beeps pulse through the room of machines.

"Hi Jim, it's nice to see you. I want to share some things with you if that's okay."

He nods his head.

"I know the Healer loves you and wants to heal you. May I hold your hand and pray for you?"

He nods his head again. I reach out and hold his hand—the same hand that violated me years before– and I begin to pray over him. I pray with my eyes open and I watch his chest slowly move up and down, his fingers twitch, then his arms and legs jerk.

"Healer, I forgive him. I release a blessing over his body.

Healer heal his body, Your creation. May his muscles and the brain function the way You created them. The Healer gave his life so that you can be healed. He has forgiven you and all that you've done, do you understand?"

Jim nods. Anne is pacing back and forth near the door.

"I can't believe this. I can't believe this," she mutters.

"What do you mean?"

"You know what I mean."

I realize she is referring to my forgiveness and compassion. Despite everything, Anne is watching forgiveness unfold.

"You're not the only victim of Jim's wrongdoings. But you're the only person to forgive him." She begins to weep and leaves the room.

I gently squeeze Jim's hand and offer him a small smile. He smiles back.

I hear the Healer's voice whisper in my ear.

I'm proud of you. This is the fruit of forgiveness and mercy, powerful healing.

Chapter 15

WILD DREAMER

For you have given him his heart's desire, anything and everything he asks for.

~ Psalm 21:2

I walk into my home office, sit upright in my chair, roll up my sleeves, and open my laptop. I flashback to my ten-year-old self typing on the vintage typewriter, I punch the keys "Once Upon a Time". It's so cliché, but I want to write it. I desire to come up with beautiful creative words. After reading dozens of kids' books, I want to write my own.

"Did You encourage me to be a writer? Did You place the desire in my heart?"

Yes! My dreamer, I want you to record all of our adventures!

I'm excited to be the first daughter in my family to graduate from high school. However, the summer after my senior year, I face the real world as an 18-year-old. I'm on my own and I need to pay bills and figure out how to make it all work. I'm afraid of falling into debt. I choose to work, and eventually graduate from esthetician school and pursue my passion in the beauty industry. My lack of a college education is a regret I'll carry for many years to come. I don't feel qualified to fulfill my dreams as a writer.

"Do You think I can be a writer?", I ask, hopefully.

You already are a writer, dear Sandra! You don't need a special piece of paper from a university to tell you what you are capable of. You've followed the dreams I put in you, just as you continue to follow your dreams today.

"I want to dream again, with my new adventurous heart! I want to partner with the dreams You have for me. I want to move forward. How do I re-learn to dream after so much heartache?"

I am the Wild Dreamer. Your heart and dreams are worth fighting for! With your new heart, I am revising and reviving your dreams. They are bigger than you can imagine!

The Wild Dreamer takes me off the map to the Glory Beach. I squish the sand between my toes and look out to sea. A wave carries a bag covered in grey ashes to the shore. I open the bag and smoke rises from it. When the smoke clears, I see burned pieces of paper among the ashes. I make out a few words on the destroyed paper: family, writer, and finding my father.

"What are these, Wild Dreamer?"

These were your hopes and dreams.

I begin to cry as my knees hit the sand. It's true. I have nothing left. The fire burned everything. My dreams died. I had dreams to write. I think about the vintage typewriter.

>Once upon a time…I found my biological father.
>Once upon a time… I went to college and graduated with a bachelor's degree.
>Once upon a time… I became a gymnast, a hip-hop dancer, an attorney.
>Once upon a time… I have a loving husband who honors me, and we create fun memories together.

My once vibrant dreams faded along with mounting issues in my family and they turned into dull ashes when my mom died. I recognize that part of me died when she did. After her death, I stopped dreaming. I stopped hoping. I only focused on the bad things happening in my life; losing my sisters, my biological father's identity, and trying to solve a murder.

I have written things down in the Letters showing you aspirations for your life. It's one thing to read it, another to have them penetrate your heart. I know the plans I have for you, plans to prosper you and give you hope and a future. I am here, so you can live an abundant life, the Wild Dreamer assures.

"A life without dreaming feels hopeless. I recognize this now. I don't want to live in hopelessness anymore."

Sandra, I am supporting you and showing you your wildest dreams. I am always at work. It is My joy to take the tragedies of your life and bring beauty from them. I am taking your dreams and I am revising and reviving them. All those things you put behind you because they didn't seem to line up with My will. You have lived in a time of disappointment. I'm telling you, it's time to dream again … it's time to dream again … it is time to dream again! I packed those dreams inside of you. You think they're your ideas. However, I am the Author of those dreams."

I wipe the tears from my cheeks and rise to my feet.

Declare what you want! Your words are powerful! Life and

death are in the power of the tongue. Declare your dreams right now, on this beach!

> I have a loving family.
> I will enjoy the journey.
> I will be present in each moment.
> I will travel and tell others about Your love and goodness.
> I will pray for the sick and see them healed.
> I will see You heal the brokenhearted.
> I will find my biological father.
> I will write, dance, and create.
> I will know You so well, when I get to Heaven I won't be surprised!
> I will see You do the impossible.

This is a great place to begin, but Sandra, My dreams for you are actually much bigger than these. I fight a good fight for your dreams. I am tenacious in bringing the hidden dreams alive. Your dreams are infinite, there is no room for boxed-in-cake dreams, or one-size-fits-all dreams. Your dreams are limitless. I love blank canvases, open fields, vast land, and I especially love going off the map, where the view is exceptional. No strings bind. The higher perspective releases probable possibilities. I love to partner with My friends in dreaming. I love to drop hints of these miracle dreams. It's how I woo My dreamers, My believers. My purpose is to engage the dream in My believers' hearts.

"How do You pull that off?"

I plant these. He opens His hand with tiny seeds.

"What are those?"

These are the dream seeds from your heart. I planted these dreams inside of you before the foundation of time. You may think they are your own doing, but it was really Me. I placed them in your heart when I created you. I release the stirring emotions inside of you, and I give you permission to dream. Dreaming is My story through you; through your eyes and your life. Remember when you dreamt of being in the beauty industry as an esthetician? I put that passion for beauty in your heart.

"It's true! I love making people feel good and beautiful," I share.

You and I are similar, I love making people beautiful too, He agrees

"I want to dream, but I don't know where to start. I have to be honest, Wild Dreamer, it's hard to dream when so many things I've desired haven't happened."

I believe it's time for you to think differently, to dream differently, and put behind you anything that doesn't line up with My heart's desires for your life.

Zephaniah talked of Me singing over you in the Letters. I have been singing for many years. I have waited for you for generations.

"Really, for generations?"

Yes, really! Your inheritance of love; I knew you would grab hold of the love that has been passed down for generations. It was available to all your ancestors before you, but you were hungry for Me. For instance, look at your high school education. You were hungry for that diploma, but no one in your family before you were hungry. You are hungry to see Me make a difference on the earth. Love has been available to all of your family members before you.

I see my generational line. I see my ancestors line the gold streets on the Other Side. I recognize some of them; my Grandma Carol, my Great Grandmother Elsie, my Grandpa Irvine, a short man who looks familiar but I can't quite place him, and others I don't recognize.

In Heaven and on Earth everyone has a choice. I don't take choices from people or force them to choose. You searched for your identity. Who are you? Who is your father? What is your purpose?

In this search, you have become hungry for more. The hunger to dream is in you. I know because I placed it there. You will be an encouragement to others. You will be invited to share your experiences fulfilling your dreams to an audience who is eager to hope and dream for themselves. You will make a difference in their lives. I will show others what can happen when you partner with Me in your dreams.

These dreams will extend far and wide. They are more than you can ever imagine. My dreams aren't just for you, they are also for the other people in your life. You can only access these dreams by talking to Me, believing in Me, and following Me. It requires faith for you to believe what I share with you. You are welcome to come here anytime and talk on the Glory Beach. We can talk and discuss all these plans I have for you if you choose to let Me into your dreams."

I ask, "It's a choice? What if I'm confused by my dreams? What if I don't understand them?"

There is always a choice. You are always free to choose to cooperate or ignore the dreams. I do not force My plan on anyone. With our connection, you can decide which dreams are impossible to achieve on your own. Those are the ones I love to bring about!

"Well, some of my desires are to have a strong family, one that leans on You. I want my family to know what You have in store for them," I share.

I want that for you, too! Continue to share your dreams with them!

"I want to travel with my friends and experience Your dreams for us as we adventure and learn more about ourselves. I want to fund mission adventures as they share Your mission and encourage others to dream," I go on excitedly.

Amen! I will show you how and when to partner with Me making these trips reality!

"I want to travel the world, sharing different Facets and revealing all the baggage You have taken from me. I want to share my story with the world!"

Then, to the nations you will go! You will travel to Cuba again, El Salvador, and Colombia. A big transformation will take place in Brazil. I will let you know when it's time to travel.

"I want to make a beautiful mark on the beauty industry with my cosmetic line!"

I have plans for your business, Beauty Decree!

"I want to share my story of what You have done in my life."

Oh, you will!

"I want to pay for my children's education, an opportunity I didn't have when I was a child. I want to be the mother I didn't have growing up," I confess.

Yes, that is a bold and challenging dream. You will face doubt and fear because you're traveling on an unknown road. But I will guide you.

I go on, "These are just some of my dreams, but I long to connect with some family members. Remember the day I lost them all? I want to find the family I've been searching for -- my biological father and my half-sisters."

I am all about family restoration! You will reconnect with them in due time. This is a great place to start. However, you will not believe what I have planned for you, even if I told you. I'm going to keep these dream seeds in this velvet pouch, you'll need them later.

"Alright, I'm ready whenever you are!"

As I sit at my office desk and stare at my computer, I look intently at the desktop's wallpaper, an image of a glorious beach, pristine sand, and calm water. I gaze deeper, taking in every pixel of the image. Feeling a peacefulness, every cell in my body is calm.

"Ding!"

I'm startled by the chime of my inbox. My eyes dart to the top righthand corner of my screen and I see a new email notification from a sender I don't recognize.

> Subject: Speaking Inquiry for the Des Moines Register Storytellers Project
> Dear Ms. Rohrer,
> We are pleased to invite you to our upcoming speakers' series. We are inspired by your personal journey and would be honored to feature you as a guest speaker..."

As I continue to read the email, I start to smile, realizing my first dream with my new heart is already coming true.

Chapter 16

BEAUTIFUL ONE

He calls me beautiful one.
   ~*Song of Solomon* 2:10

It's been years since I've traveled down Black Diamond Trail. I was only eight years old when the house caught on fire, but as an adult, the image of the charred remains is burned in my mind. I take extra precaution around Christmas time, making sure to unplug the lights when we leave the house. The smell of smoke triggers me. I never thought I'd want to go back to that country road, but now I have the opportunity to re-visit Black Diamond Trail for the first time in 30 years.

I drive my friend, Elizabeth Grace, to the old address. After all these years, the road is somewhat familiar. When I turn right onto the Black Diamond Trail, the memories flood back. We cross the narrow bridge over Old Man's Creek, and I recall endless summer days chasing butterflies and catching bumble bees. We pass St. Michaels Catholic Church in Holbrook with the tombstones next to it. We head down the giant hill and I see Tom's old house, the neighbor who broke in trying to save us. I hear he has since passed.

"It's on the right," I say looking at Elizabeth Grace.

We slowly approach the property and I roll down the window. Confused, I look back at Elizabeth Grace.

"It's not how I remember. This doesn't look right, maybe I'm at the wrong address."

The house is all wrong. The trees are all gone. The house is modern, rigid, an eye sore in the country setting. Emotions rush through my body, my heart sinks, my eyes burn. Discouraged, I look to Elizabeth Grace for reassurance.

"This was a mistake, I don't think we should have come. This isn't what I wanted to see."

Elizabeth Grace encourages me to look out the window again.

"Let's turn back, there's nothing to see here," I say defeated.

Elizabeth Grace tries to comfort me.

"I know this must be hard, Sandra. Seeing a beautiful new home built on the land where tragedy once struck, but this is what restoration looks like. This is good."

I look out the window again. The property looks so different from what I remember, except for one thing, the ditch full of wildflowers. I take a deep breath, inhaling the beauty and exhaling restoration. I nod at Elizabeth Grace and signal as I start to drive away. I look in the review mirror one last time and smile.

"You're right, it is beautiful to see restoration."

I get home and Kingston is especially excited to see me. I drop my overnight bag and he rushes to the foyer and begs me to color with him. We gather our supplies and sit at the kitchen table to start coloring. He begins another version of his favorite superhero and I begin to draw the ditch from Black Diamond Trail. I struggle to bring the three-dimensional image in my mind to the paper. Frustrated, I pivot from an idea and try drawing a meadow of wildflowers instead.

Kingston looks over at my drawing, "What is that mom?"

I try not to take my young son's confusion seriously, but I do. I'm hurt. I second guess myself. "I'm not creative," I tell myself. I put the crayon down and stare at my disaster.

You are creative.

I look up from my drawing and notice another Facet is sitting with us at the drawing table.

"I don't think I am. I'm not creative."

Who told you, you weren't't creative?

"Well, I don't remember anyone telling me I am creative. My mom was so creative, and everyone reminded me of her talent. She could use any medium to make her drawings come to life. As a kid, I never thought my scribbles got her approval. She didn't show interest in any of my attempts at art. My mom never hung my art on the fridge or featured it on her dresser with her other prized possessions. Staying home sick with the chicken pox, I made her a self-portrait. She didn't say much when I proudly presented it."

I sigh as I doodle with my crayon.

"I treasure all of my kids' pasta jewelry, popsicle crafts, and Mother's Day gifts from Sunday School. I wonder why my own mother had no interest sharing her passion with her daughter."

As I wonder this, I hear a voice deep in my soul chanting,

"You are not good enough. You are not good enough."

"What is that sound? It sounds like my voice, but I'm not saying anything."

It's your mental recorder, the tape you play in your head. You have another message you play too, 'I'm not creative'.

"I know I got the recording from believing the lie I wasn't good enough in my mom's eyes, at least that's how I felt. I replay it all the time in my mind. I compare my actions with someone else's and the lies and comparisons flood right in."

What do you want to do with that recording?

"I want to start fresh. I want to give it to You. How do I give those lies to You?"

I would love to take them, this is how you give them to Me. Repeat after Me, 'I take this thought captive: I'm not creative. I won't let it play anymore'. Let's do an exchange. Give Me the tape recording, 'I'm not creative.' I have a truth for you to hide in your heart and when the recording starts to play again, you stop it and declare 'I am creative!' How does that sound, beautiful one?

"Wait, 'Beautiful One', is what I call You. I will do it!" I exclaim.

I look over at Kingston as he continues to draw. He picks up a blue colored pencil and begins creating an ocean for his superhero picture.

Yes, that's how I see you, you are My beautiful one. As I am, so are you in the world. I have a gift I want to give you in another exchange for the recording. Look at the ocean Kingston is drawing. Look beyond the paper.

The ocean and beach look familiar. It's Glory Beach. I look intently and see something riding a large wave. The sun is reflecting off a large wooden object with metal pieces. It's a glistening treasure chest riding into the shoreline. I run to the chest. I'm curious about its contents. After unsuccessfully trying to open the lid off the chest, I notice a tiny lock. The Beautiful One opens His hand and inside is a miniature key. The bow is shaped like a cloud, and light flickers inside the iridescent yet translucent key shaft.

"It's beautiful, the key is so dainty and cute for this big treasure chest!" I exclaim.

Remember when you sat with Michelle, your life coach, and she reminded you of your value for beauty. It was an awakening moment for you. You looked for beauty all around you, realizing beauty was reflected in your home, your work, and your lifestyle. You are motivated to bring beauty around you. I want you to know whatever you create, it's always beautiful to Me. Sometimes you need the smallest of keys to unlock the biggest mysteries.

I take the reflective key and place it perfectly inside the keyhole. Turning the key, I hear a click and the top of the chest cracks open. Slowly opening the chest, the inside resembles the same design as the key.

Clouds of iridescent sparkle and light fill the chest.

"Can I touch it?" I ask in awe.

Of course. This is YOUR treasure chest.

I quickly move my fingers through the fluff. Then I feel a swirl of liveliness inside me. I see a kaleidoscope of color and texture. I pull back, and with big eyes I look to the Beautiful One.

"This is crazy! I've never seen anything like it! It's beautiful! What is it?"

It's your creativity. Creativity is beautiful and you can have as much creativity as you want, because you ARE creative. You have your mother's artistic talent flowing through you.

Suddenly I flash back to my mother's art, remembering one of her pieces titled Swallowed Key. I get the chills, and I'm reminded we all have our keys we carry around, unlocking our own and others' potential: keys of hope, restoration, encouragement, and faithfulness.

The Beautiful One locks eyes with me, *Keys were never intended to be swallowed or buried, they are meant to unlock and release. You are right. All of my children carry sets of keys. Keys are gifts to help others, and with this particular key you can have as much creativity as you want.*

I know what He's describing. I am the only one who limits myself.

Let's create and release beauty together. My beautiful one, I enjoy creating with you. This is the place where masterpieces are made. You are like Me when you create. I bring life to you, and when you create with your words or your paintings, you bring life to others. I created the earth, and it is good. It is delightful and plentiful, yet from the outside some may see places of ugliness. Creating beauty releases restoration. When you create with Me, you will bring delight to others. You will share the beauty with them. I love it when you are creative and recognize My beauty. I have more beautiful things to reveal to you. Would you like to discover one right now?

"Yes, of course!" I gleefully respond.

You know how you have always admired creativity in other people? I want to remove the comparison thief from your thinking. You can't compare your creativity with others' work. Don't look for validation from other people. I know you are creative and that is enough. I want to encourage you to shift from a mindset of inadequacy to complementary. What you value in others can be used as a tool to enhance your own gifts. When we partner together, you'll recognize the accessibility you didn't have before. That is a key I have placed in you. Those things you really admire in others hide in you. Instead, let's bring those values to the surface. Let's change the story from ugly to beauty.

"I have wanted to be creative all of my life, but I always compare myself to others and the gifts You have given them. How do we bring them to the surface, Beautiful One?"

Ask Me questions and listen for My response. When you hear My response, record it, paint it, sing it, dance it, build it, share it with others. Sometimes I will suddenly move in your heart and mind and show you. I will use dreams, sunrises, moments with your children, gusts of wind, new friends, rainstorms, new encounters with family … the list is endless. Notice when you compare yourself. Comparison robs the deposits I've made in you. The gifts in your life are irrevocable. Your gifts and talents are seeds in need of cultivation and nourishment. When we team together, an acceleration happens, and beauty reveals herself.

"How exciting! I can't wait to see what we do together!"

I look down again at my wildflower drawing and remember just how hard it is to be vulnerable and put myself out there.

"Beautiful One, remember when I started to blog? Every Monday night I cried because I was vulnerable without much response. It wasn't what I hoped for. I didn't get the response I thought my content deserved. I second guessed myself, wondered if people were judging me."

Some people will, and some people won't. Not everyone will like you. Is that okay with you?

"Not really. I want to be liked, I always have. When I was younger, it was much harder because my mom didn't show me affection. When I know I'm liked, it makes me feel good about myself. I've done a lot of work to act like a chameleon and constantly change my colors. I can read people well, almost to a fault. It's as if I can tell if they are open to my perspective or not, and I will continue to share if they are open, and if they're not, well, I just shut down."

You picked up becoming a chameleon to fit into your family as a little girl. You didn't get love and acceptance at home and you wanted to find it somewhere. When you were five years old at your grandparents' dinner table, you nodded your head, agreeing with the adult conversation happening at the dinner table. You were trying to feel accepted and understood.

"The conversation is a blur, but I remember."

This survival tool was picked up as a child, but it is debilitating as an adult. It created self-betrayal. I want you to be okay with the woman you are today.

"I don't want to hide behind something I'm not. I want to feel free to express myself without wondering what others think of me," I confide.

There might be holy chaos, but you need to trust in Me. I will submerge you in My ways, drowning out doubt. Filled with faith. Floating in forgiveness. Drenched in love. Remember, it's My mission to bring beauty from ashes. My goodness will never exhaust or come to an end. There is always more in Me.

"That's so exciting, but I have to ask, how is that so? How can Your goodness never end? How can You have endless love for me? What if You get frustrated with me?"

My patience is not like an earthly mother or father's. You will be more frustrated with yourself than I ever will be with you. I'm patiently waiting for My children, and specifically for you, to come to Me. Everyone gets to freely choose. I don't make anyone do anything. Remember when we went to the slums in Mexico?

"Yes!"

I showed you the hibiscus flowers on the ground and I gave you the idea to deliver beauty.

In my mind's eye I go back to that day in Mexico. I'm asking the leader of the group if we can stop at a flower stand and I purchase three dozen red roses. I want something beautiful to share with the people living in the slums. Our van is filled with the sweet fragrance of roses.

As you found joy bringing roses to the slums, My joy is to bring beauty into desolate areas of your heart; your marriage, your relationships with your sisters, your desire to find your father. I want to bring life to what looks dead in those places in your heart that seem hopeless. I bring red roses to the areas of your heart in need of beauty. Just like your friend pointed out your value for beauty. You are like Me when you bring the vibrance of a red rose to the dull places in a heart.

When we arrive in the poor neighborhood, the kids run to us. They all beg for the flowers. Their eyes are bright! Their faces fill with big smiles and I see how the flowers bring them joy! Their joy brings me joy. It is the highlight of my time in Mexico.

Walking to the slum I pray, "Beautiful One, bring Your life to this area."

I heard that prayer and I answered it. You are My messenger.

I look at Beautiful One and I smile.

You are My beauty in action. I want you to communicate My heart to people who don't know Me. Beauty is bringing life to places that look like death. The Mexican slum is lifeless.

"Yes, the smell is toxic. To make money, the people burn insulation to find copper."

I feel heaviness walking through all of the garbage. The heaviness in the air, like a heavy cloud over my head. I imagine hell looks similar; a void of color, only rusty orange, brown, and black colors fill the landscape.

We break into small groups offering water to the people. The area is heavy with black smoke, and the residents age more aggressively because of their rough environment. Their faces and arms are black and leathery from tending the fires. My heart breaks for the people, as their faces reveal a depravity.

As we walk, I hear the pieces of glass, wire, and plastic crunch beneath my feet. We approach a middle-aged woman with a red handkerchief on her head. She's wearing a dirty skirt and brown top. Cory, a kind quiet guy in the group, asks if he can pray for her. He reaches out his hand to take hers. She quickly hides her hands behind her in shame.

The translator chimes in.

"She is embarrassed because of her blackened hands."

"I don't care and want to pray with her anyway," Cory replies. We can all feel he means it.

I'm scared to touch her hands. The bacteriology class I took years ago speaks loudly in my head.

"Why am I so disconnected from Your heart? Why couldn't I reach out to her, Beautiful One?"

Sandra, it's important to look beyond the physical, I see the heart of people. Ask Me for help when you start to feel disconnected.

We continue our quest delivering water, roses, and prayer, and I try to take in the foreign environment around me. I catch my own judgmental thoughts.

You share common ground with them.

"Really?!" I'm shocked to hear this.

Your environments may be different, but your hands are doing the same as theirs. Your hands are busy looking for treasure in a lot of junk. You're busy scrolling on social media, obsessing about your daily workout, or counting calories. This is all junk trying to make you feel better about yourself. Instead, come to Me.

I realize, I am busy with nothing of value at the end of my life. I look for treasure among the trash, in social media, and I obsess about aging gracefully. I know I spend too much money and time on something that has no eternal value.

Your eyes are on the wrong things. Don't look for a busy life that will have NO ETERNAL VALUE. The real value, the real beauty, is in the people around you. It's in relationships.

As we leave the slum, I look back and notice a little boy walking up the hill of trash. He's holding a red rose in one hand and his dad's hand in the other. Among all the slum's dark colors, there is the treasure: love and connection.

In My eyes, they are the treasure. They are valuable. They are beauty in the ashes. Remember Sandra, I am with you, and I want to release the beauty through you, whether in words, a song, a dance, a flower, a picture, or a human connection. These are keys you release that unlock other hearts and bring restoration. These are forms of creative expression through you. I want to give you these keys. My hope is the beauty I 've put in them is discovered and comes back out of them. It's My desire that they come to My heart. Just as restoration took place on Black Diamond Trail, I want My children's beautiful hearts restored and living fully alive.

"Mom, I'm done with my picture. Look at my superhero flying over an ocean!" Kingston exclaims.

"I love it! We'll put it on the fridge. I need to add one more thing to my drawing."

I pick up a gold crayon and begin drawing the key. When I finish, I share it with Kingston.

"What do you think?" I ask him.

"I like it! My favorite part is the cloud in the key. Let's put it on the fridge!"

Chapter 17

JEWELER

You shall be a crown of beauty in the hand of the Lord.
~ Isaiah 62:3

"It's called 'The Jewel House' on 444 Heritage Road. Turn right off Grove Street and it's on the left. There is a faceted diamond heart on the sign, you can't miss it," Jen directed.

"Thanks Jen! I appreciate your referral to fix my ring. Have a good day!"

I lay my cell phone down as I parallel park at the jewelry store. I enter the double glass doors and notice the atmosphere is tranquil. The emerald shaped ceiling is eye-catching; the graduated turquoise color ascends to the center skylight. The light kisses the regal chandelier, dispersing a brilliant rainbow throughout the showroom. I feel like a jewel just standing in the store.

Immediately an older gentleman greets me. His glasses slide halfway down His nose, revealing His bright blue eyes. His face glows. It's a Facet!

Hello Sandra, I'm the Jeweler. I've been waiting for you.

"Hello! Jen recommended You to help me fix my ring and possibly design a new one. Does she know You are a Facet?" I reach into my purse and pull out a velvet pouch with a ring tucked inside.

Not yet, the Jeweler grins.

"I came here to have You fix my ring but I'm sure You brought me here for something else." Excitement fills me at the possibilities. I love jewelry. I think to myself, "This is going to be good!"

You know Me well, I have some surprises. Let's see your ring first, though.

"See, this prong is broken, and the stone is gone," I note as I point out the empty silver prong. I place the ring on the velvet pad in front of me. "My great-grandmother, Pearl, gave this ring to my mother and she gave it to me."

I see you are missing other stones too.

"Yes, it's my understanding my mother pawned the ring at one time. When she returned to the shop, the owner offered her money for the diamond. Since she was short on cash, she unfortunately agreed, leaving the ring without the stone, and the prong damaged from the unprofessional removal"

Indeed, that is unfortunate. This piece took quite the journey. Do you want to start a new one? He smiles.

"Yes, I guess I do!" I say, returning the smile, "I want to honor the remaining stones and start a new journey!"

Are you interested in adding some new stones? Stones bring a new story, replacing those that have been lost.

"Yes, that would be amazing!"

I will design something beautiful for you.

I know just what you like. Let Me put this in the safe and I will begin working on it later.

The Jeweler returns from the safe with a key in His hand. Now, I want to show you some other things I have been working on behind the scenes. I'm taking you into the heart of the Jewel House, your family's jewelry is stored inside.

"What? My family's jewels?? I don't think we have any family jewelry. This jewelry is all that's left."

I know you are not aware of the other jewels, this is why you are here.

The Jeweler presses down on the gold and marble handles after unlocking the double doors. I follow closely behind him. Entering the Jewel House is like immersing myself in a jewelry box. Luxurious velvet lines the walls. Diamonds and pearls hang from the chandelier, doorknobs, and line the floors. Everywhere I look is an array of sparkling color and exquisite beauty. The glorious light reflects off the jewels, as my eyes try to follow the bouncing light from one iridescent piece to another.

"My friend didn't tell me about this part of your shop!"

Not everyone accepts My invitation. The invitation is open to all, but only those who take Me up on the opportunity will be delighted.

"I'm glad I accepted the invitation!"

He points to the crowns elevated on cushions, lining the velvet jewelry box.

There is a process to mining beauty. You are in process too. You will get revelation today in your innermost being. It takes work to refine beauty, and people may give up before the big reveal. I take delight in designing, restoring, repairing, and admiring the beauty I create. I have one stone in mind I want to show you. Every stone needs polishing; even the most striking diamond needs refining.

Off to the side, the Jeweler walks to a simple, stunning crown sitting on a velvet pillow. Its rubies catch the overhead light. The crown is familiar to me.

See this crown? He asks as He carries it over.

There is something in the way He carries it. I see the love, preciousness, and admiration for the crown. The crown has six rubies surrounded by gold laurel leaves. It's the same crown The Baggage Taker gave me.

This is your mother's crown.

I stand in silence with my hand over my mouth.

"This crown that keeps reappearing was my mother's?" I can't believe such a beautiful thing ever belonged to her.

I designed this one for your mother. The golden laurel leaves represent the victory of her children. Her children are the six rubies.

"Wait, six? She only had five children."

No, there was a child you didn't know about.

"You are telling me that my mother had another baby?"

This one died in her womb. She was 20 years old. It was after she had you. I want to show you something. Look inside this ruby.

I can see inside the jewels. Inside each one I see life. The first life I see is a four-year-old boy.

This is Matthew.

My eyes light up. "He's so handsome with those crystal blue eyes."

My plan for Matthew was to be a veterinarian. I created him with a big tender heart to help all of My animals.

I watch as he plays with the animals on the Other Side. He runs all over and then in exhaustion he plops down. The black terrier licks him. Then I see a girl in another jewel. I recognize her immediately, it's Erin.

When you look into the jewels, you are seeing My heart for them.

The Jeweler looks inside the stone with me. As we watch Erin play, descending a slide, I notice the Jeweler is looking at her with love-filled eyes. Erin stops playing and waves at me, blows a kiss, then takes off laughing.

It was My plan for her to enter and exist on earth. It's My plan for you to reunite with her in Heaven.

We look into the next jewel, and it shows my brother Jason. He's bending down in a mud hut. He is praying over a boy. I see a banner over Jason that says, "Overcomer". Jason continues to talk about his dreams of traveling abroad for missionary work.

I gaze into another jewel, seeing my twin sisters as the Jeweler does. They are torch carriers, united and leading the way for others in their generation to see the Facets.

I adjust my eyes to the last stone, my stone. I'm gathering jewels, sharing my discovery of the Jeweler with others. I'm telling everyone how important it is to honor one another and the virtues the Artist has placed in each person. Then I see myself crying, hoping they all accept the invitation of the Adventurer. The Jeweler brings us together for a purpose.

I wipe my eyes, "It's beautiful to see through the Jeweler's eyes".

Please come this way. He leads me to another crown.

I have a piece that needs your help. This is a crown belonging to your Great Uncle John, your grandmother's brother. This crown represents his fatherhood. This crown is his heart, and his treasure is within these stones.

I admire the crown. "It's amazing, how could it possibly need any of my help?" I pause then see there is an empty prong. A jewel is missing."

Yes, this is where I need your help. Do you trust Me?

"Yes, I trust you. These stones really see the truth."

This will challenge you, but I know you can handle it and I need you to trust Me all the way through.

With a deep breath, I accept the challenge.

I want you to check your Ancestry account.
My mind immediately races to my biological father.
"Oh my goodness, will I finally find my biological father?" I ask excitedly.
I check the website daily, each time wanting a viable lead. I pull up my account, and I notice I have a new relative, a woman who looks like my mother. My heart drops, I'm disappointed. I was hoping I'd find relatives from my father's side. I shrug it off, but decide to message her anyway:

> Hi Nancy,
> You look just like my mother. How are you related to
> Sue Kersten?
> Sandra

I receive a response.

> Sandra,
> Thanks for contacting me... I've been thinking about you all day and what I would say if you were to message me. Yes, I see that we're closely related... out of all the matches I got through Ancestry, you are the best match! I am looking for a man named John. I am hoping you can help me fill in a few blanks.
> Your relative (of some sort),
> Nancy

I instantly respond:

> John is my great uncle. Can we cut to the chase? Do you think you are his daughter or sister?
> Sandra

> Sandra,
> I believe I'm his daughter, that is, if the information fits

together like I think it should. John worked at a drug store with a woman named Cecelia. Cecelia is my mother. She worked the cosmetics counter. I don't talk about this with her, so the details aren't all there.
Nancy

I can't believe Nancy (at 53 years old), is also looking for her biological father. It's strange to think I've had more of a relationship with my Uncle John than his daughter. I begin to think about my own biological father. He's somewhere out there and he might not know about me.

I quickly respond to Nancy.

> Your profile picture looks like Uncle John. I'm sure you are his daughter, you look just like him! Do you know you have five half siblings? I too took a DNA test because I am looking for my biological father. Please let me know if there is anything I can do to help.
> Sandra

> Sandra,
> I've heard conflicting stories, we will have to ask him! It's my understanding I was the secret no one knew about. I grew up knowing I was adopted. I was the youngest of five siblings. However, I didn't know until I was twelve my adopted parents were really my maternal grandparents. My sister was really my mother.
> Nancy

> Nancy!
> Wow, what a story! Did your mother tell you when they split up?
> Sandra

> Sandra,

Well, what I've been able to piece together is that my mother just upped and left. John went to my mother's house looking for me and my grandfather told him to never come back. That was it.
Nancy"

Nancy,
Wow! So, he might not know you exist!
Sandra

Sandra,
Nope, I don't think he does. What can you tell me about John?
Nancy

Nancy,
Uncle John is always smiling. I've never seen him grumpy. He is my mom's uncle, making him my great uncle. John and his wife divorced after being married 47 years and they had five children. So, you have three brothers and two sisters! He's warm and loving and a good father to his kids. I will connect with you on social media so you can see them. Would you like me to call him?
Sandra

Sandra,
Yes, that would be wonderful. I'm afraid an out-of-the-blue call from his long-lost daughter may startle him. I don't want to scare him off.
Nancy

Nancy,
Of course, that makes sense. I will give him a call.

Sandra

I'm surprised how nervous this phone call makes me. The phone rings and sure enough Uncle John answers.

"Uncle John, this is Sandra. How are you?"

"Well, not doing too bad."

"Have I caught you at a good time?"

"This is as good of time as any." He says with a jovial voice.

"Alright, are you sitting down? A couple of years ago, do you remember when I called you, asking questions about my biological father?"

"Yes, I recall that."

"Well, in my search, I did a DNA test through a website, and a woman recently popped up as my second cousin. I didn't recognize her as a family member I knew. I reached out to her and asked her about our common ancestors."

"Okay…" he says slowly.

"Her name is Nancy and she believes she is your daughter."

There's a pause, silence on the other end.

"When you worked as a night security guard, do you remember a woman named Cecilia? She worked at the same Jewel Osco drug store selling cosmetics."

"Kind of. Sandra this was over fifty years ago for me to recall, but yes I think I remember the gal."

"Well, that is Nancy's mother and Nancy believes you are her father. She looks just like you! I can send you pictures if you'd like. And if it's all right, I will give her your number. I will let you talk to her and figure out the mystery."

I notice Uncle John seems sideswiped with the news.

"I will need to think about what you are saying and have blood work done to prove it. I appreciate the call, Sandra."

"Oh Jeweler, I would give anything to be in Nancy's shoes and discover my biological father. It's one thing in my life that is impossible! I can't move away from it even when I know I've got to move on. I know you placed Roy in my life before I was even born. I'm so grateful for him. He brought me into his family and provided for me. As a pre-teen, he encouraged me to work things out and not run away from my problems. He would not let me quit when things got tough. He encouraged me to push through. But I still want to know where I get my dark brown hair and skin from, and whose brown eyes match mine. There's a part of me that feels missing. That's what makes this so hard, Jeweler. You led me to Nancy, and I've helped her with the one thing I want for myself for over thirty years."

I know you and I know this is a desire of your heart. I know this goes deep, and I want you to keep praying. I don't want you to remove this heart's desire. I placed it in your heart. It is My will for people to know their parents and their families. You are no exception.

"Oh, but the injustice wants to creep in. I want to stomp my feet and yell, 'It isn't fair'! This is what I want! I lost my mom; can't I at least find my father, Jeweler?"

I take a deep breath. I will refuse those thoughts. I will feel joy that Nancy and John found each other. Nancy texts me later, mentioning she spoke to John for the first time on July 17.

"I'm so happy for them, Jeweler. It is the kind of ending I want."

Are you ready to place the stone in John's crown with Me?

"Okay. From deep in my heart, I'm elated for them. This is how it should be. Nancy's search is over, and she is finally restored to her biological father."

I know it's difficult for your heart to see what you've always wanted, and to be a part of restoring the jewel to your Uncle's crown. I want to show you yours. Your crown is beautiful, each stone carries a story. I know what you've been through and what it took to bring light and brilliance to those places that were dark in your life. Here is a canary diamond. It is double the size of the others. This represents a double increase of joy to match each trial you've gone through, the jewel of overcoming! This crown represents your ability to overcome your personal hardships and tragedies. You allowed Me to break through all the facets of what you've gone through to reflect My light. This is a breakthrough moment. You're allowing Me to shine through your heart.

As I look into the canary yellow diamond, I see myself laying this crown at His feet.

"It's only because of You that I have the strength to overcome. Only You know what I've been through and the depths of healing power and the mining of the jewels in the ashes."

Exiting the Jewel House, I survey the beauty one more time. Tucked in on the side, I see what I didn't see before, a crown with the word "Father" sitting on the workbench. Tools are in place. A polished stone sits beside the crown ready to be added to its other jewels.

Before bedtime, I pray, "Holy Spirit hover over me while I sleep".

In my dream, I am holding a manila envelope. Written in red on the outside of the envelope are the words: Don't let her see this! She must never know!

I realize the information I've wanted to know my entire life is in this envelope, the identity of my biological father. I will finally find out. Then I wake up.

Awake and in my bed, tears slide down my face. I have wanted to know everything about my biological father. If he is still alive, what does he do for a living, what impact has he had on the world? How we are similar? Do I hold my silverware the same way he does? How do I act like him? Why am I having this dream? I let this go. Yet, I want to know everything! I can't fall back asleep. I'm too wound up, so I grab my phone off my nightstand.

While checking my phone, on the DNA website, I see I have a new relative, Jonathan. We share 444cm of DNA. This is a 1-2 cousin probability. I wonder if he is a maternal or paternal match? I click on the common ancestors button. According to the website he is not related to anyone on my mother's side who has done DNA testing. But I don't know for sure, his last name sounds Polish. I think Polish ancestry would line up with my mother's blue eyes and blonde hair. I'm sending him a message.

> Jonathan,
> Welcome to DNA testing! I see we are cousins; do you know how we are related?
> Sandra

"Jeweler, will I ever find my father?"

Chapter 18

Gardener

Those who sow their seeds with tears will reap a harvest with joyful shouts of glee.
~ *Psalm 126:5 TPT*

It's springtime and I am headed to Oklahoma to work. I'm thankful I still have clients who want my facial services. It's great to work a few weeks here and there, and it's nice to return home and be a mom.

It's a long drive, but I enjoy road trips. I love the Flint Hills. I love looking at the sculpted land and contrast of colors, rivers, hills, the animals. I make a quick stop at a gas station to fill my car and upon returning, I drop my keys by the door. When I pick them up, I see a Facet, the Gardener.

Hello My darling Sandra. Beautiful drive isn't it? I have something special I want to show you on our way to Oklahoma.

"Wonderful, I need some company on the drive. I love traveling, Gardener, but I was getting lonely."

I know.

"You speak through the land. I know You show me Your

beauty and majesty with sunsets and mountain peaks."

I love to speak to you through nature.

"Well, I enjoy it when You do. It helps the drive move quicker."

See those wildflowers over there?

"What?! I didn't realize Oklahoma had wildflowers. In the nine years I lived here I never saw wildflowers!"

This state is known for its red dirt, but there are also these beautiful native wildflowers. Similar to the sunsets you love, the Black-Eyed Susan, or the yellow Buffalo Currant, and the Triangle-Leaved Violet are all beautiful native wildflowers.

See that road ahead? Take a right on the gravel road.

"What do You mean?" I wonder as I slow down to turn.

I will do a new thing in your heart. Just like these beautiful red, yellow, and purple flowers spring up in the dry land, there are dream seeds and desires in your heart that have been dormant. I will water the dormant dream seeds. Remember when you were in Cuba you had no wi-fi on your phone? You wanted to listen to music on the beach. While you took in the waves and scenery, and one song—among the hundreds of songs— dropped down from the cloud for you to listen to.

"Yes, Redemption Rain was the song!"

I will release a redeeming rain on the dry places of your heart and water the dream seeds.

We drive to the top of a hill. I see lush grass, a meadow of wildflowers, a pond, a woodland garden, and the Gardener's house.

Follow Me. I want to show you how to garden. One attribute of gardening is patience. Timing is a big deal to release a symphony of flowers. I planted the seeds but now it's time to see beauty.

"I need intervention. I've gone a long time without seeing intervention in my life. There are areas I've longed for with my whole heart."

I begin to dig up weeds. I recognize them from the purple bag: tough marriage, finding my biological father. I look at the weeds representing my mother's murder case. That is buried, I don't mess with that one anymore. I throw the weeds in the compost pile.

Let's take a closer look at these weeds.

"But they're just weeds, there's nothing to nurture."

I disagree, let's take a closer look. The weeds have benefitted the compost, making the soil more rich and nutrient-dense. When you gave Me the bag full of weeds, it gave Me the opportunity to grow something good out of the lies. We will work this compost into the ground. It will help other plants grow in the flower bed. This past winter when you thought I wasn't tending to the garden, I was busy dreaming over you.

I smile. I love that.

"Sometimes in my life, I sense You are with me, but I don't know if You're doing anything."

The Gardener laughs. *No Darling, I'm designing, planning, and creating a masterpiece for you.*

"I'm relieved to hear that. To be honest, sometimes I feel You forget about me and my garden. When my marriage isn't going well and my life seems taken over by invasive weeds, I get overwhelmed. I don't know if You're there to help me pull them. I want to grow with my husband and children; I want our family to bloom. I share the same desire for my sisters, my brother, and Roy. I desire to find my biological father, and justice for my mom. I have all of these seeds tucked in my heart, praying something comes from them."

Remember, I'm always at work. You may not notice because I work behind the scenes until the timing is right. Look at this apple tree for example. What does it take to grow an apple?

"Well, the obvious elements: sun, water, and rich soil."

Yes, and you are missing something important.

Tapping my lip with my finger, I contemplate the Gardener's words. Out of the corner of my eye I see a large bumblebee. He lands on the apple blossom and flies off.

"A bee?"

Exactly! When the bee pollinates the blossom, the fruit creation begins. Just as you were on the hunt for them on Black Diamond Trail, I have sent bees into your life.

The thought makes me tear up.

"Of course. You've sent Marian, Michelle, and Elizabeth. They've made a huge difference in my life."

I sent them to you, and I've sent you to them! It's cross pollination, Dear Sandra.

"It is! I love them dearly. They have invested in me. Each have shown me Facets of who You are and worked through them. I really wouldn't't know You, or even be able to communicate with You, if it weren't for their loving examples introducing me to You. Thank You for bringing those bees into my life. You designed them and placed them in my garden beautifully."

Follow Me. I'm taking you to the garden house.

We start our walk through the woodland forest. Among the trees are delightful yellow tulips, sword ferns, and mossy rocks. Following the trail, we walk through a canopy of trees. At the end of the canopy stands the garden house. The house is a simple white house, black shutters, and a large sliding door.

The Tear Collector brought Me some beloved vases. I specifically want the vase containing the tears you grieved for your mom.

He walks inside and returns with the vase in his hand. Nestled close to the garden house is an unseen garden from the pathway.

I have purposely placed this garden close to My home. It is special and I take delight in the meaning of the garden. It's your heart's desire garden.

I'm stunned. "All these years and You care about all of my heart's desires, everything I've held onto?"

Yes, I will show you. What seeds do you want to plant?

I want to plant the seed of resolving my mother's death.
I want to plant the seed of finding my biological father.
I want to plant the seed of a great marriage.

He pulls out a velvet pouch, unties the cords, opens it, and reveals three seeds.

I know your heart and I know these are the seeds you've wanted to plant. How many tears have you shed over these three seeds?

My eyes well up with more tears.

"Too many to count."

I know every tear you've ever shed, and the Tear Collector gathered them for this moment.

"What are You doing with the Tear Collector's vase?"

Let's begin planting your heart garden. Let's take these seeds and place them here along the side of the garden. I've prepared the ground. This is the hidden work you haven't seen Me doing. Let's plant this seed of resolving your mother's case. Pack this nutrient rich compost around it lightly.

My eyes widen. The thought of resolution almost seems impossible. I've waited almost twenty years to find this resolution, and when I let it go with the Territory Taker I concluded there may not be any here on earth.

This one will have a huge impact, so we need to give it a lot of space to grow. Next, we have your family seed. This will flourish. Let's place this seed towards the front of your heart garden. I want it to be close so I can guide it as it grows. The final seed represents daring hope to find your biological father. Before we plant this seed, I want you to renounce the lie 'I will never find my father'. Remember when you said those words in your heart? Your words matter and your words created a barrier. You made a vow in your heart. It's time to pluck the lie out and plant this truth, 'You will bring him to me'.

"I renounce the lie that I will never find my father. I pluck this lie out of my heart. I embrace the truth, You will bring him to me!"

Take a pinch of the glistening hope and blow it over the seed. Even if it's years later, it's important to remove lies and replace them with truth. The truth is worth planting. Truth enables you to release freedom in your life and bring awareness when another lie enters your garden. Pluck the lies immediately. Your tears of being faithful, your tears of perseverance, your tears of love, and your tears of longing fill this vase. I will move them to the watering can and pour out your tears on your dream seeds. In different seasons, these heart desires will sprout, grow, and produce a harvest.

"How will I know when to harvest?"

You must be patient. You must not come back and dig up what we have already planted. You need to nurture and pray over the seeds until the plant flowers or bears fruit. If you do these things, I promise, you will have a harvest.

The Gardener takes the watering can and pours my tears over the seeds.

None of your tears were in vain. They have meaning. They have purpose. Your tears matter. I speak life over your dream seeds. May they grow and unveil truth to you!

The awe of His love is overwhelming. I never thought anyone cared when I cried, or about the desires in my heart.

"I know my tears were never wasted. However, today You have shown me they are precious and purposeful. Thank You for sharing this with me. I love that You not only honor my tears, but You use them to flourish my dream seeds."

The following week on the drive home to Iowa, I stop at the unseen garden looking for growth. There is nothing. I am disappointed to see nothing has sprouted. I thought we made so much progress, I figured I would find something in the supernatural garden.

The next day it rains. The Gardner comes out of the house smiling.

Here is the redeeming rain!

It's summertime and Karis and I are in the backyard harvesting basil for dinner. My phone rings. It's Lt. Rogers, he's worked my mother's case for years.

"Hi Sandra, how are you? Hope I'm catching you at a good time."

"Hi Lt. Rogers, yeah of course I'm in the backyard with my daughter. What's going on?"

"Well, I'm calling because I approached a producer from a television show. It's a series hosted by a successful female prosecutor. Her team works with local law enforcement to close cold homicide cases. They've made several dozen arrests and convictions. I approached them because I think your mother's case might have a shot. With their help and access to more resources, we might find your mother's killer."

I'm speechless.

"Sandra, you there?"

"Yeah Lt. Rogers, I'm here. I don't know what to say. That's good news, but how would it work? Would my family be involved? Would we have to pay them?"

"No, you wouldn't be responsible for anything along those lines. At this point, I'm not sure how involved your family would be. I'm not even sure if they will take the case. I planted a seed with the producer. I'll let you know if I hear any news."

"Oh, okay. Thanks for the call Lt. Rogers. I need to think about it. Honestly, I've closed the door on that part of my life. I'm not sure I'm ready to re-open it."

I hang up and put my phone back in my pocket.

"Who was it mom?" Karis asks.

"It was Lt. Rogers. He suggested involving a television show to re-open my mom's cold murder case, in the hopes of getting an arrest."

"Mom, I know you have waited a long time. I will pray something happens." Karis states with certainty. "I'm going to bring the basil into the kitchen."

"Ok sweetie, thanks. I'm going to stay out here a little longer and pull some of these weeds."

I walk to the shed looking for a small shovel and garden gloves. As I walk in, I see the Gardener.

How are you feeling after that phone call?

"Oh Gardener, I am in shock! When the Territory Taker gave me the weapon of letting go and then experiencing supernatural peace in the car, I thought it would be the end of it. I'm afraid. I really don't want to lose peace."

Who says you need to give up the peace you once so willingly received? Continue to walk with Me on this trust journey.

"Yes, I will keep peace moving forward!"

Will you trust Me when things don't look how you think they should?

"I believe so but help me if I don't!"

Contact Lt. Rogers.

Instead of texting him, I decide to call him.

"Hi Lt. Rogers. Let's go for it."

"Great, Sandra. I'll confirm with the producer and be in touch."

Just as I start to think it's too good to be true, he texts me.

"Good news! I heard back from the show's producers. They want to take on the case! We will start filming in July."

It's been a few weeks since I've talked with Lt. Rogers. The producer instructs me to arrive at my brother's house in Williamsburg.

I pull up to the filming location, and instantly I'm brought back to the morning after her death, almost twenty years ago. Instead of police cars surrounding my mom's old trailer, I see black SUV's filling my brother's driveway. Walkie talkies holler instructions, hand-held cameras are everywhere, there are cameras on tracks, all kinds of people milling around. I thought this would be a small ordeal. I was wrong.

The producers give us little direction except where to sit. They are kind and they reassure my brother and me, trying to calm our nerves. I'm excited to share the healing journey I've encountered over the years.

In my mind I practice what I'm going to say, how I will share my experiences with the Facets. Unfortunately, I quickly learn that the producers are more interested in my brother's pain. They are curious to learn his perspective as he struggles to move forward with his life. They invite him to sit next to Kelly, the show's host and lead investigator, and ask him to share his story of struggling to move forward. Disappointed, I try to keep my head up and feel grateful for this opportunity to hopefully uncover the truth and find justice.

"Oh Gardener, this is so hard."
You've waited nearly twenty years for this moment. I know you can wait one more week.
It's been one week since we visited with investigators. I get butterflies with anticipation. I go through both scenarios in my mind. I want to be okay, to keep the peace, even if they don't make an arrest. On the other hand, I want justice and this case to be resolved.
Trust Me.
"I'm trying," I say with hesitation.
The concluding interview is at my brother's house. I ask Josh and Elizabeth to come with me. As we drive, I stare out the car's window remembering one year ago (almost to the day) I attended Bill Kietzman's retirement party. I completely surrendered and finally felt the peace and courage to let go and move on. So much has happened in one year, and here we are about to discover who murdered her. I hear the Gardener's voice.
This happens when you use the weapon of letting go.
After friendly exchanges, the producers encourage us to sit

down on the couch and the cameras roll.

I finally hear the words I've waited for almost twenty years.

"We were able to get an arrest warrant for Jerry for killing your mom."

Absolute gratitude overwhelms me. My heart squeezes tight.

"We got him mom! He will be held accountable for what he did to you. I knew he did it!"

Relief sweeps over me. I don't realize how much I need this resolution.

"Thank You, Gardener, for bringing resolution to my heart."

I look at all the faces on set.

"I really want to thank all of you for never giving up over the years. I cannot tell you how thankful I am to bring this to an end."

The following day, July 17, 2015, 19 years and 10 months after my mother's death, I get the long-awaited phone call.

"Sandra, Jerry is in handcuffs, in the back seat of my car. He is charged with first degree murder for the death of Sue Kersten, and the judge will set a one-million-dollar cash bond."

"Thank You." It's all I can say. Over half my life I've been waiting for that call.

Tears fill my eyes as I walk outside to my backyard garden. I look up at the sunny sky, and out of nowhere I feel raindrops fall gently on my cheeks. Redeeming rain. He is crying tears of joy with me. I think to myself and smile, it's finally over.

Always remember to Trust Me, Sandra. Especially if things aren't what they seem.

Chapter 19

COMPASS

Give God the right to direct your life, and as you trust him along the way you'll find he pulled it off perfectly.

~ *Psalm 37:5 TPT*

"Sandra? Hi, I'm Melissa, the secretary for the Johnson County Attorney's office. A plea deal has been reached and we would like to have the family come down on Wednesday, Feb. 15 at 8:00am. Will this work for you?"

My heart starts racing. "What did they agree on?"

"I'm sorry ma'am, I just set up the meeting. The attorneys will share that information when you arrive on Wednesday."

"Alright," I hang up the phone and pace the floor with my hand on my head. "Oh goodness a plea deal, nineteen months have passed since the arrest. It's happening like You said, Compass."

I'm calling Bill Kietzman, the retired DCI agent. I bet he has more insight on the plea deal. Anxiety fills me.

"Bill, do you think the charge will be second degree murder?" I start pacing again.

"I don't think so. It will likely be a voluntary or involuntary manslaughter charge."

"WHAT?! It CAN'T be manslaughter. I want him to be charged with murder, because that is what he did. He killed her! He hit her, he burned her, and he covered it up. Voluntary manslaughter would be an aggravated misdemeanor and only up to five years in prison."

"You need to prepare yourself, voluntary manslaughter might be the charge."

"But I'm not okay with manslaughter, it's so unjust what he did to her. Manslaughter would…" I trail off, I can't even imagine if he is charged with manslaughter. "It would mean less time in jail." Distraught, I hang up. I can't believe it.

Wednesday comes too soon. My brother and his wife, Roy, Josh and I, and law enforcement, all sit in the courthouse conference room. Jessie, one of the assistant county attorneys, begins the meeting.

I'm taken back. All this time I've been talking to Dawson, the other assistant attorney, I thought he was in charge. This is disappointing. I've been talking to the wrong person! Jessie goes right to the point.

"We have come to an agreement with the defendant and his defense attorneys."

I sit on the edge of my seat. Was my worst fear coming true?

"We've agreed to let him plead guilty to the following charges. Second degree arson because we have overwhelming evidence found at the defendant's home that he set your mother's body and car on fire, and an additional charge of suborning perjury. While awaiting trial, he sent a letter trying to buy someone's alibi. And lastly, even though the defendant was charged with first degree murder he will be sentenced for one count of willful injury."

I gasp. Willful injury? Shock flashes on my face.

Jessie continues, "We also agreed to the Alford Plea which means that the defendant does not accept guilt or responsibility for the three charges, but acknowledges that state prosecutors have substantial evidence to secure a conviction for three offenses if this had gone to trial. He will be sentenced to no more than 15 years in prison. The state of Iowa immediately cuts the sentence in half. The state of Iowa will double the time he has already spent in jail. Bringing his approximate jail time to four years."

My mouth drops, my lips start to tremble, and hot tears of anger and sadness slide down my cheeks. Oh, my goodness, this is worse than I ever imagined. She was heinously beat, burned and a car fire was a cover up to her death. He won't even accept responsibility? Why would the prosecuting attorneys agree to all of this injustice?

So, I ask, "Why didn't you agree with manslaughter or second-degree murder, or even take this case to trial?"

I want answers. This is a mess, this isn't anything close to a victory.

Jessie answers, "After twenty years, gathering evidence has been difficult as we look at an upcoming trial. Some evidence has been lost and damaged."

"What evidence has been damaged?" I ask in disbelief.

"The previous county attorney had your mom's vehicle destroyed because he was tired of paying the bill for the impound."

My watery eyes become angry, how could evidence be destroyed? This case never closed! Jessie continues, very matter of factly, "This doesn't make the prosecution look good, so this situation wasn't in our favor."

"What about her autopsy results? Her head trauma?" I ask, surely believing they are overlooking something.

"There has to be enough evidence filed away somewhere, or the television show couldn't have encouraged an arrest."

"Unfortunately, the state medical examiner lost some of her X-rays. He had a few offices across the state, and we don't have the files anymore."

It feels like blow after blow of bad news.

"Also, the medical examiner has some credibility issues a few years ago" Jessie added.

"What about all the testimonies of her friends and his friends?" I demand. "An acquaintance of Jerry's interviewed on the television show. She said he knew how to kill someone and make it look like it was an accident."

I share this with my brother and dad since they hadn't seen the show. They were called to testify in court and the attorneys didn't want them to be biased after watching the show, so they were court ordered not to watch it.

I keep thinking of the two words: willful injury. Two new words that pierce my heart. This new heart is bleeding. I sit in the conference room, looking at a collected group of detectives and family members who waited 20 years for this horrific news. I sit and fold and unfold my tissue. I'm speechless. It's all so unexpected. I naively believed truth and justice would prevail, only to be squandered by a plea deal.

I need to call Bill. I start dialing his number.

"Bill?" I can barely say his name through all of the tears. "Bill, the attorneys agreed to one count arson, one count suborning perjury and one count…"

I move the phone away from my mouth because I'm trying not to cry into the phone. There is silence on my end.

"Are you there?" Bill asks.

I try to find my composure while wiping my tears.

I cry, "Yes." I continue, "It's not even manslaughter."

I have to move the phone away again. I hate these two words. "It's... willful... injury." I push the words out. "It's an assault charge."

"What a travesty, I'm so sorry Sandra."

In anger I add, "How can I wait over twenty years for an assault charge? It's so wrong!"

"I wish this turned out differently. You get to have your say with the victim impact statement. Voice your thoughts in the courtroom. Don't be a snot, but be firm."

I hang up the phone and decide I'll start working on my statement. I'll make another statement to the press, too. I'll no longer be silent to appease people. I've been quiet all my life.

The assault charge, the destruction of evidence, lost evidence, the lack of care or concern from attorneys … goodness, the Johnson County Attorney wasn't't even involved in sharing the plea deal with the family.

I wish I could wash my hands of this. These lawyers move on with their lives not realizing how much their decisions affect ours.

"Compass, I need direction. I need help processing this. I need to write a victim impact statement and a statement for the press. What will I say?"

I will give you the words. I will help you as you write, and I will teach you what to say. I will help you speak.

"Yes, I want You to help me. I have too many feelings right now. I'm angry, I'm sad, I feel I've been treated unfairly, even betrayed by the justice system, my mother wronged yet again."

I open my laptop and begin to type.

It's the day of the plea bargain, the collected agreement of all involved attorneys. I sit in the courtroom at the Johnson County Courthouse observing the small room. The judge sits in front of the court, the Assistant Johnson County Prosecuting attorneys sit in front of the judge on the left side of the courtroom, and the court-appointed defense attorneys and the defendant sit in front of the judge on the right side of the courtroom. The jury box sits to the right of the attorneys.

My focus shifts to an earlier conversation I had with Lt. Rogers. "When you walk in, sit in the jury section."

The jury section? That's ironic. Unlike the jury, we have no say in his plea deal. I find a seat in the jury box, take out my victim impact statement, and tuck my purse under my seat. I wait with my other family members for the judge to begin. The Compass sits next to me.

"How has it come to this, Compass? I never wanted a trial. I knew they would scrutinize my mother's character, because she made some poor choices in life."

You are not your mother's keeper. She made her own choices. It's not your place to control how people see her.

"But this is not how I wanted it to end either."

Sandra, I understand you're upset, Jerry will receive a weak sentence. A sentence you have no control over.

"This is so hard, Compass. I need direction. I feel like I'm spiraling out of control."

She is in the cloud of witnesses watching. You are not alone in this Sandra, I am with you.

My husband, best friends, my mother's sisters and brothers, all file into the small courtroom. Jerry enters shortly after. He takes his seat, keeping his head hung low. He's dressed in an orange jumpsuit; his hair is long and scraggly.

How does he look to you?

"Absolutely awful. What happened to him? How did he end up in this place of his life, Compass? Give me Your eyes to see what happened."

As we sit in the jury box, the Compass invites me to follow Him. My mind's eye takes me to a room. I see Jerry as a baby. His eyes are sunken in, his skin has a grayish hue, he's wailing, he's so upset. Anyone could look at this picture and see this baby isn't valued or cared for, just left on his own to fight. In this picture I can understand he is disconnected from the very people who needed to teach him how to love, how to care, how to value.

"What a terrible experience he had as a child. Everything makes more sense. I feel sorry for him, compassion overtakes my heart. I have Your heart and it hurts for him doesn't it, Compass?"

This picture of his childhood doesn't excuse him for your mother's death. But this opens your heart to pray for him. Pray he will turn his life around so he will allow Me to fill those places in his heart that weren't met by his parents. This is very important, Sandra, no person is too far from My reach. Jerry allowed evil into his heart, but it doesn't mean it can't be removed if he ever desires a heart change.

"I'm glad You showed me this, Compass. It's not all reconciled in my heart, but I believe a shift has started in my mind; a shift to seeing Jerry how You see him, through compassionate eyes. I'm trying hard to process what is going on, but it's all happening so fast. We've waited over twenty years for a process that all unfolds today."

My thoughts are interrupted by the bailiff, "All rise, the Honorable Judge Kennedy."

Reality sets in. I am in a courtroom with the man who murdered my mother. They are announcing his sentence today. I can't believe this is the end. This is unbelievable. I thought my mother would receive the justice she deserved like in so many cold case tv shows, movies and songs. I thought my mother's story would join them.

I whisper, "I'm sorry mom, I'm sorry this is how your story is unfolding."

"Compass, why did we veer in this direction?"

People have free will. I don't control people. But I'm going to turn this situation around for your good.

My mother's sister, Fern, stands from her seat and reads her victim impact speech. Her last sentence ends with a sentiment some of the family secretly all share, "I hope you burn in hell."

My brother reads his statement. Then, it's my turn. I'm glad I'm last to speak. I walk through the family in the jury box to the witness stand.

From the corner of my eye, I see the Territory Taker.

You are brave and unafraid. Look him in the eye and share from your heart.

I stand firmly, looking at the courtroom in front of me.

"Would you please state your name for the record?" Judge Kennedy asks.

"Sandra Rohrer."

"And what is your relationship with Ms. Kersten?"

"She was my mother," I reply.

"Go ahead."

With tears in my eyes I address the courtroom and read the statement I prepared.

"My mother, Susan Kersten was a beautiful person, an amazing artist. She was highly creative and a free spirit. There are no words to express the void I have in my life because she is not here. Her life mattered to me. On September 24, 1995, I was 19 years old when Jerry took my mother from me. Jerry stole some of the most important relationships from me. I lost my family. He took my sisters away when they were babies. I was part of their lives and when my mother died, he packed the girls up and left with them. He promised me he would let me see them, and I was allowed to see them once. That was over 20 years ago."

I look around at my family's faces with red eyes and continue.

"I've lived longer without my mother then with her. I was not given the opportunity to say my goodbyes like some do when they know someone is dying. Jerry took that from me. It hurts the most that she is not here with me and there is not a future with her in it."

Looking at my husband I continue.

"Her grandkids don't know her. She doesn't get to celebrate their birthdays. I can't take my kids to visit grandma. I can't even have coffee with her. I also lost the opportunity to learn who my biological father is. I saw her the night before she was murdered and asked if she would draw me a picture of him. She never had the opportunity. That's four relationships taken from me by Jerry."

"It is devastating that my mother's death was ruled a homicide, but her death won't be resolved today as one. This sentencing has shaken my faith in the judicial system because this is a twisted form of justice… he got away with murder today because he is able to plead guilty to willful injury."

I look at Jerry, "Although my mother was your victim. I am

not nor will I ever be your victim. I will not give you the power of ruining my life. And I do not wish you harm, Jerry."

I pause and continue my gaze at him. I hear Compass whisper in my ear.

Are you going to tell him? Love can win right here if you will allow Me to show mercy through you.

Then I see all of them, all the Facets of the Heart of God are standing in the courtroom.

The Territory Taker moves forward and declares, *This is new ground to be taken, to show mercy to him even though he deserves judgement. You are brave!*

The Tear Collector holds the vase of my newly collected tears, *I know this hurts, but your tears are powerful.*

The Adventurer pipes in, *This is an invitation to Jerry to see My goodness and kindness.*

The Baggage Taker picks up a piece of black luggage, *Give me the lie, forgiving him makes it okay what he did to your mom.*

The Wild Dreamer holds up keys, *Forgiving Jerry will unlock your heart and dreams.*

Beautiful One, shining bright, nods His head as He shares, *I will create something beautiful from this.*

The Healer moves His hands from His heart, *This will bring healing to all who hear of this moment.*

The Weaver interjects, *This moment will be woven from My*

heart, to yours, to Jerry's, to each one in this courtroom, and beyond these four walls. I will weave good into this terrible situation.

The Wall Shaker releases an iridescent dust over Jerry, and I see the fortress he built with his own thoughts blocking his heart. Then the Wall Shaker says, You can help Me shake this wall around his heart with your words.

The Jeweler, surrounded by brilliant green light adds, *You are an overcomer. This emerald stone will be placed inside your crown, a token of how proud I am of you.*

The Gardener pulls out a pouch of seeds, *From these seeds of forgiveness, you will harvest joy!*

Hearing each one of the Facets, I realize I have all the encouragement, love and support I need to move forward. I turn directly to Jerry.
"Do you mind looking at me, please?"
He doesn't move an inch.
"Jerry, will you look at me?" I plead.
The defense lawyer turns to him whispering, "You don't have to look at her." And he doesn't.
It's okay, move on. He doesn't need to look at you to receive My words. Can you share what you really feel?
Looking right at him with his eyes looking to the ground I continue.
"Well, I want you to know I forgive you for hitting her, I forgive you for dousing her with gasoline and lighting her on fire. I forgive you. That's all I have to say."
Gasps fill the courtroom. The intensity of my words impacts everyone in the room. My Aunt Fern cups her mouth.

Moments earlier, she wished he'd burn in hell and I was publicly forgiving him. There wasn't a dry eye in the jury box.

I'm so proud of you! You did what few could do. You took the ground you had once given over to the Enemy of your soul. You spoke truth. You confronted fear and death and on the Other Side is your voice. Your voice is your weapon. Using your words to shift hearts and atmospheres. That is what I call you to do, bring healing with your words to set the captives free.

"I feel every Facet of Your heart. I feel empowered to share my heart. If I hadn't had Your heart, I wouldn't have been able to do it. I feel lighter and know I am a daughter of purpose. My purpose in this moment is to forgive and set the captive free."

Judge Kennedy settles the courtroom. "Does the State have anything further regarding sentencing?"

"No, Your Honor," the Johnson County attorney replies.

The judge looks at Jerry's defense attorney, "Mr. Rimes, do you have anything to add?"

Mr. Rimes reiterates his original statement. "Your Honor, the only thing I'd like to ask is that you follow Rule 2.10, and to not sentence our client to an indeterminate term that does not exceed 15 years."

Judge Kennedy nods his head and looks at Jerry.

"Jerry, this is the time in the hearing you can say anything you want to say, anything at all, although you're not required to say anything. Is there anything you want to say?"

Jerry keeps his head down.

"No thank you." He whispers. His face is masked by scraggly grey hair.

No, thank you? I couldn't believe it, it was hard to swallow. No regret? No emotions? Nothing?

The Gardener reassures me.

It's okay. Your words are seeds. Your words of forgiveness you spoke to him won't easily disappear from his mind. I will bring them to remembrance.

Judge Kennedy looks at Jerry and shares his decision.

"I've carefully considered this case. As counsel has stated, this is a plea agreement under Rule 2.10 and, therefore, my choices are to either accept the plea agreement you reached and sentence him to that agreement, or to reject the agreement and allow the defendant to withdraw those pleas and proceed to trial. I agree to the plea agreement both parties have reached, sentencing the defendant to a maximum of 15 years in prison. The defendant is adjudicated to be guilty of the offense of willful injury resulting in serious injury, the offense of arson in the second degree, and suborning perjury.

Jerry, while I sentenced you under the plea agreement reached between you and the State as I'm required to, I think it's important you continue to remember that your actions have had extraordinarily awful consequences. The actions you took for which you've now been convicted are obviously incredibly serious, devastating, and frankly, just downright stupid. As a result of your actions, as we heard today, kids were left without their mother, other family members and friends were deprived of their relationships with Ms. Kersten, and society as a whole has been deprived of gifts and contributions she could have made. And to add insult to injury, while others suffered, while others waited, while others did without, you walked free for twenty years living your life."

And just like that, with those words, the Judge's gavel hit the wood and the sentencing was over.

I let the Judge's words sink in. It seems as if my words only affected the judge.

He is the only one to have empathy for my family, the

charges initially filed, and the outcome the attorneys agreed upon. He understood we suffered and waited, (and maybe) he would agree this conclusion is disappointing.

The Weaver comforts me.

I know your expectations were for a different outcome. I will work this out for your good, I will give you understanding.

The crime victim advocate looks at our family in the jury box and asks me to answer a few questions from the press. I begin to read the press statement I prepared.

"Hello, I am Sandra Rohrer. I am Susan Kersten's daughter. I am completely disappointed by the sentencing today. Before I go further, I want to acknowledge law enforcement and how I appreciate all that they have done on their end to gather evidence to bring justice for Susan Kersten.

"My mother was brutally murdered on Sept. 24, 1995. I believe Jerry struck her and killed her. He moved her body, and he staged a car accident, and when it didn't work, he doused her with gasoline and lit her and the car on fire. I am completely baffled by the Johnson County attorney's office and their agreement with the defense. This is not an act of willful injury. This is murder. I have never been more devastated by two words in my life. This outcome doesn't reflect the charges initially filed. They ruled my mother's murder a homicide in 1995."

I take another deep breath and continue.

"The Johnson County Attorney's office did not ask our family for feedback on the plea agreement. I'm extremely disappointed Jerry pled guilty to willful injury, arson, and suborning perjury, there is no admission of murder. I reiterate none of the charges he plead guilty to today account for her murder.

"Plain and simple, this is not justice. This resolution shows the brokenness of our legal system. He killed her and this plea doesn't reflect the heinous crime. My mother never deserved to die. This makes my mother a victim twice. Once by Jerry and again by the legal system. Jerry got away with murder."

I pause and look up at the press. "Thank you."

Roy approaches me and gives me a hug.

"I'm so proud of you."

Walking out of the courthouse I feel the chains drop. My head is up. I faced one of my biggest fears and I wasn't scared. I said what I really thought, I didn't hold back. I am free. I finally feel the freedom I've longed for years. This is it. It's really over this time.

You have learned to trust Me. I'm so proud of you, Sandra.

As I walk away from the Johnson County courthouse, I look back at every Facet I have met along this journey. The Tear Collector, Wall Shaker, Weaver, Healer, Beautiful One, Adventurer, Baggage Taker, Wild Dreamer, Territory Taker, Jeweler, Gardener, and my Compass. For once in my life, I realize I needed all of them to wholly heal my heart. There is one last place I want to visit with a new perspective.

I drive into the Oakland Cemetery in Iowa City, my mom's last physical marker on earth. I'm holding a beautiful bouquet of flowers from my garden and I wander through a number of graves looking for her headstone. I find it and stare over her grave. She shares a resting spot with Erin. My mother and sister were human beings of purpose. I pause in stillness.

"Thank you Mom, for being my mom. I love you and miss

you."

Take time and remember her and all the love she brought into the world.

Love waves wash over me. There are so many memories with her: making gingerbread ornaments, watching sunsets, her pregnancy (with twins!) news, playing gas station as a kid, watching her paint the Eugene Ely piece, applying purple eyeshadow on me for the first time at 13 years old, encouraging me to start a makeup business, enjoying irises alongside our farmhouse, making my first Thanksgiving turkey for her even though she was a vegetarian—so many good memories that cancel out the bad ones.

I gently lean the flowers next to her headstone.

"I'm sorry this isn't the ending I wanted for you, but he was found guilty for hurting you, and he won't spend much time in jail. However, this is it mom, it's finally over."

I walk away from the grave site with resolve, finally an ending to this harrowing journey.

Chapter 20

Daring Hope

He was so kind, so gracious to me! Because of His passion toward me, He made everything right and restored me. So, I've learned from my experience that God protects the child-like and humble ones. For I was broken and brought low, but He answered me and came to my rescue.
~ Psalm 116:5,6 TPT

The reality of the whirlwind of last week settles in, I sit on my sofa staring out the big window of my living room. In my head I keep living in the memory of the words, "willful injury".

Healer, I'm having a hard time with all of this. I can't think of those two words without bawling.

I know this is really tough on you. But, you are going to get through it and with some time you will see this differently.

"It's so hard," I say moving to the floor to lay face down. I curl up in a ball and start to cry.

These tears are precious.

The Tear Collector gathers my tears and cries with me.

"I'm so confused," I confess. "I thought You encouraged me to go on with the television show so law enforcement could re-evaluate the case. I thought You would finish this. I thought the bad guy would be held accountable. I'm still so disappointed."

Weaver chimes in, *I know this looks like a mess, but I will show you something beautiful.*

"I don't want to see it. I'm mad! I don't want this to be how it ends. I'm completely devastated, all I can do is cry. If this is how life is, then I want to die. I'm done, this is so disappointing. You had the power to change this and You chose not to! I feel like I'm back where I started. I don't know if I can trust You."

I call my friend as I drive to get lunch at the fast-food restaurant down the street.

"It's been two weeks since the sentencing and I struggle to leave the house," I say with a nervous little laugh. Quickly, I realize it's my turn to give my order. "I need to let you go, I'm going through the drive thru."

"I'd like a #10 meal."

"Okay, you can pull around and I will give you the total."

Taking my sandwich and drink, the cashier hands me the receipt, $7.17.

"Oh, my word! Stop showing me that number!" I say with gritted teeth to the Facets. I became aware of the number when Jerry was arrested on July 17, 2015.

I went back to the memory where 717 was first brought to my attention to the day, a year before. And a few days after the Territory Taker gave me the weapon of letting go. My friend,

Angie, and her husband, Alejandro, pray for me and he looks at his watch. It shows July 17, 2014 at 17:17. He decides it can't be an accident. He sees the numbers at the right time. He looks up the biblical significance of 17, it means overcoming the Enemy and complete victory. The number stands for victory. I remember Alejandro telling me it takes 17 muscles to smile.

I recognize the calendar icon for the iPhone is July 17. And, not to forget my passport expires July 17, 2022. Then there's the time I waited in line at the car wash and the truck in front of me had a license plate with the last three numbers 717. I notice hamburger meat priced at $7.17. For a year and half before the plea deal, I can't evade the number after the arrest. I know the number represents victory, but that's not what happened with the plea deal. It wasn't a victory.

I wad up the receipt and throw it in the paper bag.

"Why would You do this?" I question Compass. "If You direct my steps, why this devastating blow?"

Sandra...

"Just stop. Don't talk to me. I want You to leave me alone. You don't care. If You cared about me, You would have intervened. You knew I cared how this ended. And it looks like You don't. I'm done talking with You."

I roll in my misery for days. I can't take care of my children. I abandon work. The pain in my heart is excruciating. Not only is it not going away, but something intensifies the pain. I feel heaviness in my mind again. It's familiar, I've been here before. I am tormented. I see pictures in my mind's eye. A metal wire around my neck getting tight as I sit with a wall of offense in front of me. With each bitter thought the tormentors tighten the wire. The wall I built with my resentment and disappointment muffles any words. I have isolated myself again and I can't hear Him over the wall I have erected.

I don't know what else to do, so I call Bill. Surely, he will have encouraging words. He wanted justice as much as I did.

I utter my pain.

"This is so unfair, and I can't believe this is how it ends."

After my long rant Bill interjects.

"Wow, are you done? You sure are being negative."

Quietly, I reply, "I guess you're right."

"I don't know if you see this, but you are making this all about you. You are not the victim, your mom was."

I'm stunned. What a slap in the face.

"It's about your mom and her choices."

No one but Bill could have said this to me. Not my husband, not a friend, no one in the family. He earned my respect and I know he cares, and I know he's right.

I get off the phone and slump on the couch, realizing I became exactly what I told Jerry I wouldn't be; his victim.

So where do I turn now? What do I do? I can't go on like this. Then I see it, a piece of baggage with "INJUSTICE" written in big letters. The injustice bag is intertwined with the victim mentality bag. It's easy to pick up both at the same time. I got rid of the victim mentality baggage once. I can't carry them again, it's too much.

Staring at my bedroom ceiling, the words of the disciples come to mind, "Where else can we turn Lord, who has the words of eternal life?" Then I hear a whisper,

Your life is not your own. You were bought with a price. You were bought in love." The words spark life within my heart.

"You are the only One who has words of life, and what I'm experiencing is death in my heart. I surrender! I'm sorry! I want You in my life. I want to hear what You have to say."

With those words, the Wall Shaker tears the wall down

and I see a brilliant light from a distance. It continues to come towards me, and I notice the radiant light forms a heart. The Heart of Light comes towards me and I can see His face … Jesus' face.

I see all the Facets within His heart. The Tear Collector holds the bottle of tears, the Weaver intertwines good from the bad situations, Wall Shaker blows iridescent dust onto the wall of my heart, Healer ministers forgiveness into my heart, Beautiful One has a bouquet of roses to release beauty and restoration, the Adventurer waves me into the nations of the world, the Baggage Taker disposes my lies, the Wild Dreamer unlocks the treasure chest of my impossible dreams, the Territory Taker prepares the weapons to keep the ground, the Jeweler polishes a crown, the Gardener speaks life and releases redeeming rain, and finally My Compass points directly to Jesus.

Truth hits my heart, "Jesus, you are my Daring Hope."

"My hope is in You. You have shown me Your nature and who You are by revealing the Facets of Your heart to mine. I know You!"

Jesus' words of peace flow.

My child, you have come so far. I'm proud of you. Thank you for allowing Me to work in your heart. I knew you would heal. Life and death were set before you, and you chose life.

"Your words are life, agreeing with You is life, being obedient to You is life. You sent the Facets to help me see your heart and know who you are! Now, I realize that carrying around heart baggage is death, lies are death, the victim mentality is death. I know this is truth. I agree with You. You're right, my life is not my own. You bought me with a price. Your blood. You died to give me life. I surrender, I give my life to you! I don't get to say how it looks to be okay. I will trust You."

Look at Me.

I can't muster the courage to lift my head.

Look at Me. I have something for you. Take My hand in yours.

I reach for His hand and we dance in the night sky. The stars are sparkling on the black velvet background. The clouds move to the sound of His voice and He begins to sing a sweet, familiar melody.

"I know You care about me. Don't You want the truth to come out? Where were You when the plea deal was decided?"

When I ask, He shows me how the scene unfolds.

I see Jesus talking to the defense attorneys as they are working on the case. They don't want to hear the truth.

His truth.

Then, I see another scene. This time Jesus is talking to the Johnson County attorneys. There are piles of cases stacked on their desks. The office is overrun with cases and chaos. I see Him talking to them and they have their hands stretched at His face not wanting to hear the truth.

I begin to cry.

"You were there, Jesus!"

They didn't want to partner with truth. They have their own agenda and plans, this is their way of working out justice. This isn't My kind of justice.

"What is your kind of justice?"

My justice looks like forgiveness. When mercy triumphs over judgement, My love wins. In My kingdom, justice looks like forgiveness and forgiveness is justice. I want you to know, love won in the courtroom. You have a choice too, if you want to see My perspective.

"I do."

There is an earthly courtroom and a heavenly courtroom. The Johnson County courtroom on February 17 was the courtroom on

Earth. Two thousand years ago there was another courtroom in Heaven, that's where love won. I offered forgiveness for all the times you carried hatred in your heart, for all the lying, manipulation, living in doubt, and hidden motives in your heart. I didn't give you what you deserved. I showed you kindness and mercy instead of judging you for your shortcomings and sin. I did it for love. Love kept Me on the cross. Love is why I came down. Love covered over a multitude of sins. Love causes you to overcome.

This is the emerald stone in your crown.

Jesus shows me the unfinished crown.

You overcame it all because you didn't allow yourself to become a victim. You overcame by not allowing hate to rule your heart. Through your brokenness, My light shines through your heart and impacts others. I'm proud of you My overcomer, you are My delight. I chose you first on Newport Beach years ago. Thank you for re-surrendering your life and choosing Me again. Now, I want you to focus on My eyes. Don't be distracted by the surrounding flurry, keep your eyes on Me."

My eyes lock with His. I am present. I am safe, and I know everything will be okay even if I don't see the end of the story. His eyes impart peace to my heart, and I can finally rest.

I decide to listen to one of my favorite podcasts. In this specific episode, the podcast host is referencing Revelation 2:17. 2:17 caught my attention because it is also the date of the sentencing. The verse is about a trial. The host elaborates on someone giving the accused either a white or black stone at the end of a trial based on the verdict. This hits so close to home.

"Jesus, is 717, a reference to one of your Letters?"

I grab the Letters and skim through different parts. I look through the Psalms, and Isaiah, and then turn to Revelation 7:17, and right there in little print is the victory.

> *"For the Lamb at the center of the throne continuously shepherds them unto life, guiding them to the everlasting fountains of the water of life. And God will wipe from their eyes every last tear!"*

"Yes, this is the true victory! Being with You, Jesus! All the tears I cried, You collected every single one. You will wipe them all away until one day they will cease entirely. On the Other Side there will be no more pain or heartache, or things to process and work through. I will be satisfied with complete joy and peace in Your presence. This is the fullness of Your victory!"

I leave my marketing office to meet with Ashla for lunch. Even though I've been self-employed for twenty years, I'm just learning the art of networking. I initially met Ashla at a Chamber of Commerce event for business professionals. She suggested we stay connected and help one another.

Ashla is an insurance agent and brilliant networker. My small company has such a niche and I'm struggling to figure out how to connect with new customers. Ashla shares her simple strategy.

"It's all about getting to know your customers, really show them you care for them."

I'm taken back.

"This is how successful business works? Truly care for your

customers? That's it?"

"Yes, that's it. Tell me your story. What made you who you are today?"

I hesitate, Does she really want the answer? I feel comfortable with her, but I haven't shared my story much.

"My story is pretty intense," I begin to say. "I'm not even sure where to start."

"Don't believe the lie your story is too much for people. You'd be surprised how much people can handle."

So, I tell her my story of transformation and redemption, I spare nothing. After I finish, I watch her reaction. Her eyes fill with tears and I realize my story impacted her heart.

"God is in your story. It's valuable and needs to be shared. He has healed you, Sandra."

I nod and then share with her, "You know, I told Him six years ago that if He healed my heart, I would tell the world. I would go to the nations and tell everyone".

Ashla lifts her water glass to toast in agreement.

"Well, then, it's time to tell the world."

"Amen to that," as we clink our glasses.

"Ashla, thank you for coming tonight! You know I wouldn't be here if it wasn't for our conversation months ago."

I'm backstage at the Des Moines Register Storyteller's Project feeling excitement and nervous anticipation.

"Of course, I wouldn't miss this for the world!"

She reveals her "Release the Roar" t-shirt. It's a lion, drawn by my mother. I created it to honor my mother and raise money for women of domestic violence. Creating the shirt represents so much to me: my mother, finding my own voice, women helping other women share their personal stories, and my own personal journey. I was a shy, afraid, and insecure child. Over time I've learned to become bold and brave, just like the lion on the t-shirt. He is fierce and He is always watching me, protecting me.

"Okay, I better take my seat! Break a leg, I'm so proud of you. You're finally sharing your story."

"Thank you, Ashla."

I take a deep breath, and smooth out the wrinkles on my skirt.

"It's my pleasure to introduce Sandra Rohrer, our next speaker at the Des Moines Register Storyteller Project. Sandra is an Iowan who forgave her mother's murderer when he was arrested twenty years after her death. Sandra is here to share her personal journey overcoming tragedy while searching for her identity. Please put your hands together and help me welcome, Ms. Sandra Rohrer."

The auditorium booms with applause. I say a quick prayer under my breath, "Jesus, You are true to my dreams and You have honored what was always in my heart."

I walk on stage to an audience of 1,200 people and release my roar. For the first time, I'm sharing my whole story and the daring hope I have tucked inside my heart that I will find my father someday.

Chapter 21

FATHER

Jesus said to her, "Daughter, because you dared to believe, your faith has healed you. Go with peace in your heart and be free from your suffering!"
~ *Mark 5:34 TPT*

It's Easter weekend 2020. It's been six months since I spoke at the Des Moines Register Storytellers Project. We're in the midst of a global pandemic; schools, churches, and businesses are closed, and we are encouraged to stay at home as much as possible. The news blares in the background, "50,000 cases of the Coronavirus have been reported. People over the age of 65 with pre-existing health conditions are considered high-risk."

Again, I'm checking the DNA testing websites for a DNA match after finishing the first re-write of my book.

I wish Jonathan would get back to me. He is a very close match; the website shows him as a second cousin! I wonder if he is on my paternal or maternal side, I think to myself.

A moment after that thought, I get a notification from Jonathan.

Whoa! I've never had a thought answered so quickly! In my

experience reaching out to people, I've come off too strong so I try not to appear desperate ... even though I am! I decide to wait to respond until the weekend.

Interestingly, Saturday morning rolls around and I receive an email from Eric Schubert, a 19-year-old DNA Detective. Eric had been on television nine months earlier, and I had reached out to him to see if he could help me find my biological father. He had been inundated with requests at the time and couldn't take my case, but now he can!

> Hi Sandra,
> I now have time to help you with your genealogy search if you want my assistance.
> Eric

I quickly draft my response, knowing the timing of these situations cannot be coincidence.

> Eric,
> Yes, I would very much appreciate your help. I've received an email from a relative today. His name is Jonathan Lipinsky, a second cousin. I'm trying to figure out if he's on my maternal or paternal side.
> Sandra

> Sandra,
> From preliminary research I believe he is on your paternal side. Give me some time to dive deeper and learn how you are related.
> Eric

My hands are shaking, and I have a feeling Eric is going to find my biological father. It's not even an hour later when Eric emails me again.

> Sandra,
> I've found Jonathan's first cousins. I believe one of them is your biological father. Jonathan's father, Larry, had a sister, Pauline. Pauline was from Poland and she married a Portuguese man from Cape Verde, an island off the coast of West Africa. His name is Oliver Frank. The couple had four boys and I believe one of them is your father. That would explain your DNA matches from Southern Europe and Cape Verde.
> Eric

The email takes me to the floor. A pool of tears soaks the carpet. My 32-year search for "Why my skin is darker?" ended in an hour!

I finally know my ethnicity! I know the name of my grandfather and grandmother, Oliver and Pauline. I know why my eyes and hair are brown. I know why my skin is darker. Oliver is Cape Verdean. Waves of thankfulness push the tears down my face. I have an answer to the question, "What is your ethnicity?" I am Portuguese!

I wonder if Jonathan can reach out to one of the Frank brothers like I did for Nancy? I decide to email him through the DNA website.

> Jonathan,
> Thanks for the request to share DNA a couple of days ago. I am hoping you can help me. I'm looking for my bio father. My mother died when I was 19. She never told me

his name or ethnicity. So, if this is too messy for you, I understand, but that was my intent when I had my DNA tested. I want to find this missing puzzle piece to my life. I am working with a DNA detective and he believes we are related on my paternal side.
Sandra

Sandra,
I will sincerely try to help you! I will try my best to figure this out but it's going to depend on whether my cousins are willing to cooperate. They both have families and wives, so I have to navigate those waters. However, I have a hunch which brother it is. I will try to get some answers for you.
Jonathan

Jonathan,
I appreciate you helping me! I'll give you my cell number to text with any news.
Sandra

Easter weekend is over, and the wait is tough. All the emotions are surging through me: nervousness, excitement, joy, and thankfulness. Finally, my heart's desire is so close!

I reach out to Jonathan on Monday.

"Have you contacted anyone?" I text in anticipation.

"No, I haven't reached out yet. Just trying to figure out how to proceed. I found some pics, I will send them!"

Jonathan sends a pic of himself, my grandmother Pauline (who I learn went by the name Tessie), and one of the Frank brother's son, Will.

I'm fixated on the picture. I slowly scan every detail. Tessie is fair skinned, blue eyed, dressed in a tailored mint green suit with a string of pearls around her neck. She looks like a real classy woman. And Will looks like my youngest son, Kingston! They have the same face shape.

Another picture comes through of Jonathan, Bill, Frank, and Will, standing by a body of water.

Bill has the same balding hair line as Roy! HA! He looks like Roy with his sunglasses on. I can't see his eyes though. My first thought was that he looks grumpy. Again, in this picture Kingston resembles Will.

Jonathan sends another picture of Oliver sitting at a table dressed up, holding a water glass. The picture looks like it's from the 1950s. I'm mesmerized, I can't stop staring.

There I am.

I see myself in Oliver. His eyes and eyebrows are amazing! This is the man I got my complexion from. I learn he lived to be 95 and died in his sleep, the exact way I want to go.

"Can we talk on the phone?" I text Johnathan.

"Yes, give me an hour and I will call you later."

The phone rings, "Jonathan, this is so crazy, I blurt out. I will tell you the little information I know. I was conceived around September 1975 in New Orleans. My mother said my father had a yacht and dressed nice and was in town for fun and business. The mutual connection between my mother and father was a man named Jimmy Brown, who was in the trucking industry. And that is really all I know. I don't have a name, a state, or picture. I have nothing."

Jonathan shares, "Between the Frank brothers, here is what each of them did. One of the four Frank brothers passed at 68 years old and I don't believe it was him. One brother was a ship captain later in life. Another brother was in the military. The now eldest brother, Bill, worked in the trucking industry, owned a large boat, and out of all the brothers, he was a clothes horse."

"My mother once told me when I was dressed up that I looked like my father. Bill seems to match the little information I have. Do you think out of the four brothers, Bill could be my father then?"

"I'm not sure but I'm leaning that way. I will reach out to Bill," Jonathan says with a little confidence.

I wonder, did I get my love of clothes from my father? I flash back to my mother's statement of disgust, "Sandy, everyday isn't a fashion show." I laugh, I know I didn't get my love of clothes from her.

A week passes without confirmation and my impatience is getting the best of me.

I hear dreadful words in my mind: "You are a product of a one-night-stand. What will everyone think of you? You're a mistake. You are so selfish. You are going to ruin families; even your relationship with Roy and Jason." My excitement fades to fear. "You are going to dig up the past and hurt people and families. You better stop this before you make a mess!"

I hear His whisper, *These are the Destroyer's words. Don't listen to them.*

However, my mind starts ping ponging between fear and faith. I've wanted to know this for 32 years but...

What if...
    -Bill rejects me and doesn't accept me?
    -Bill becomes angry and I exposed something shocking?
    -Or he doesn't remember my mother or the situation?
    -I'm the product of a one-night-stand?
    -His wife doesn't take it well?
    -He doesn't think I'm worth getting to know?
    -And what if this hurts my dad, Roy?

I can't continue the search. I should just be thankful I know my ethnicity and the names of my grandparents. This is amazing information to have.

I text Jonathan.

> Me: I have thought it over and I do think it's Bill. However, to be upfront with you I'm mulling around if I should let this go. I don't want to hurt people or their relationships just because I selfishly want to know.

I pause and then decide not to send the text message.

I decide instead to reach out to my friend Michelle about my dilemma.

I get her up to speed and then share my heart, "Michelle, I don't think I should continue my search. Shouldn't I be thankful I've discovered my ethnicity and leave the rest alone? It's such a risk. It's such a risk to my heart."

"Is that what you want to do?" She questions.

"Well, no," I say sheepishly.

"Who took you on this journey? People need you to finish this no matter the ending—and you need to know!"

I get off the phone with Michelle.

I close my eyes and open them to my favorite place, the Glory Beach. The gold, glittery sand, is composed of all His thoughts of me. Radiating faceted hearts are nestled in the sand along the shoreline. My eye gravitates to the magnificent gems. The hearts create a trail. I lean over to pick up the one with dancing light inside. As I stand up, I see the feet of Jesus. I jump up in joy. He embraces me and envelopes me with His extravagant love.

I hear you have quite the dilemma. I want to introduce you to someone. Sandra, this is My Father. He's behind you, and He's gone ahead of you.

Thoughts fill my mind of what He looks like as I turn around. I smile when I see Jesus looks like His Father. His Presence releases peaceful light and tangible love. I don't see my assumption of a two-foot-long white beard, half-bald, or long boney fingers to call me out when I mess up; only His eye of love staring at me.

Jesus says, "Enjoy the Remembrance Shore."

The Father and I are face to face.

Hello My Beloved Daughter. You have been through a lot but I'm going to turn everything around for your good. Let's take a walk on the Glory Beach. I want to share My heart with you. I want to solidify some things in your heart and mind about who I am. You have read about Me in the Letters, you know Me in your mind, but I'm going to cause you to think differently about Me as a Father to you. My goodness is going to shift your mindset to see Me differently. You held on to the mindset that you are an orphan, but you have not been left fatherless.

I know in the natural, you lost your biological parents, but I want you to see along this Remembrance Shore, I've never left you alone to figure things out. I've always been here for you. My love for you kept Me alongside you. I love you with the same love I have for my Son.

Let Me show you.

Clear heart facets in the sand release beams of light above the beach, creating a screen. I began to watch my life unfold. From my first breath of air, to every happy event, tragedy, and mess I created – there He was, Father God.

You see, daughter, you're not an orphan. I've always been here. I've cared about all the things you've cared about. If it mattered to you, it mattered to Me.

I see Father in different parts of my life protecting, providing, crying, and laughing with me though out my life; from my first cry when I entered the world to watching me type out my story.

"You have!" I'm lovestruck. All the cells in my body embrace the love and revelation that my Father has for me, Sandra.

I want to reveal some good things I have for you and show you times I was leading you behind the scenes. Let's look at this 'Facet of Remembrance' with the dancing light.

I grin as we peer inside together.

I see the night dream I had about the manila envelope with my biological father's information inside with red words printed, "She must not know! She can never find out who he is!" I see myself holding it and thinking. I've wanted to know this my entire life!

This dream was an intervention. I didn't want you to stop searching for your biological father. The words in the red on the envelope were the Destroyer's game plan for you. He didn't want you to know your father. You had let this go at one time and I wanted you to pick it back up. I took the Destroyer's plan and turned it into a good plan. In your search for your father, it led you to Me, your Heavenly Father. Look at your journey…

I turn around and see all these beautiful Facets in the sand. Bathed in love and mercy-filled light, the illumination flickers and jumps off of them, creating a radiant sea in the sand, glistening from the light inside Father.

I created a trail of Facets to lead you to Me. I used all the mystery surrounding you to draw you to Me and My heart. I made purpose from the heartache.

Father reaches down and grabs a turquoise Facet of Remembrance. See this one? We gaze inside behind the glow where I see myself worshipping at a Four-Wall Church.

Remember I whispered in your ear, 'I will bring him to you.'

"Yes, you did!"

We walk farther down the Remembrance Shore.

Look at this one. He holds it eye level for me.

The date "2008" is etched inside.

I see myself at a Four-Wall Church meeting and a godly man tells me, "What you thought was never going to happen is about to happen." The only thing I could think of was finding my biological father.

Remember, I shared the secret, "You are going to find him."

"Yes! Of course, that was Your voice! At the time I didn't know if it was my imagination or Your voice."

He picks up another and brushes the gold sand off.

Inside the faceted ruby was the memory of Roy telling me my mother died and I see myself pounding the floor.

"Look there You are!" I point, "You were there!" I shout with my hand cupped over my mouth in disbelief. You saw and heard me! I will never forget that moment. Wait, what is that heinous bug looking thing on my shoulder?"

I've always been by your side.

That bug is the Destroyer. He subtly deposits in your ear, 'You're never going to find your biological father.'

"That little bug said that? And that's all the bigger the Destroyer is? I thought it was my thoughts!"

No, he disguised his voice to sound like yours. He is not creative.

He copycatted your voice and planted a lie to destroy My plan for you.

"I've been deceived! I thought he was large, scary, and intimidating, yet he can only disguise his voice! Wow! I gave him way too much credit and power."

The Destroyer only wants to destroy, kill, and steal My will and plans I have for you. All the tragedy you experienced was the Destroyer's plan for your life—never Mine. All the accusations, condemnation, shame, and lies; he is the source of them.

"Yes, You are too good and loving to do those horrible things to me. I would never do those things to my kids either."

With a sparkle in His eye, He says, *Let Me show you another moment.*

"I'm in the Garden."

You renounced the vow with the Gardener, 'you would never find your father'. Breaking the vow allowed Me to replace it with My plan.

"Yes, I remember!"

Your words have authority. It's important to remember who I say you are! Let's start with your name, Sandra.

Your name in Hebrew means 'she is brave'. You are My brave and courageous daughter. When I made you, I made you with the intent you would walk where people are afraid to walk. I put that in you!

My sweet daughter look how far you've come. You are a warrior. You have faced intense difficulty throughout your life. You have processed so much pain. You invited me into the dark, raw places of your heart and mind. Every time you hear your name, I want you to think of this! Keep on being brave! It will bring you great rewards!

I am orchestrating this for your good. My timing is perfect. I write the best stories! I want the best endings for My kids. This is good news! Believe Me when I say I'm a good Father. I want you to be brave and finish this search.

"Okay. I change my mind. I will be brave. I will follow Your leads and pursue finding my father. I trust You. You have been good to me. You know how much this means to me. You have been with me through it all."

I receive a text later that night.

Jonathan: I'm going to call Bill and speak with him.

"Okay, Father, I'm trusting You! I didn't even tell Jonathan I changed my mind that I do want to find my father! I put this into Your hands."

Weeks pass...

"Father, is there anything I need to do on my end to speed this up?"
Call your dad, Roy and brother, Jason.
"Alright, I will do it. You realize Father, I'm being courageous by doing this. I wanted to wait and tell them when I knew for sure. But I will listen to You."

I call my Dad, Roy. "Hey Dad, how is it going?"
"Good, what's up?"
Nervously I start, "Well, I have a crazy turn of events to tell you about. A DNA detective narrowed my search down to four brothers. I also discovered my ethnicity; my grandfather was Portuguese. So, I now have an answer to all the ethnicity questions I'm asked. I want to let you know I've also been talking to Jonathan, a second cousin on my paternal side. He is

going to contact Bill, one of the Frank brothers, for me."

"Wow! I'm really excited for you, this is great news! I know you have wanted this for a long time. I told you all that I knew about Jimmy Brown and I'm glad you will get some answers. I'm truly happy for you."

"Thank you for being happy for me. I was nervous about what you would say. I'm really excited to see what comes of this! Thanks Dad!"

Alright—now to let Jason know. I look up his number in my contacts.

"Hey Jason, it's been awhile. How is everything?" I say in a nervous voice.

"Things are okay, taking care of kids, doing art."

"I'm calling because I want you to know I think I found my biological father."

"What?! That is great!" He says in excitement.

"My search is narrowed down to four brothers. But I believe I know which one it is. Who gets excited one of four men could be your father? Me!" We both laugh.

"Wow, Sis, I'm excited for you, honestly. You will have to keep me posted."

"Of course! Have a great day!"

The next day I decide to text Jonathan.

> Me: Did you get a hold of Bill?
>
> Jonathan: I just talked to his wife, Candy.
>
> Me: And….
>
> Jonathan: I explained everything and sent pictures. I had the wrong number for Bill. Candy was really, really

empathetic about your situation.

Me: Do you think for sure Bill is my father?

Jonathan: He just about admitted it to me!

Me: He remembers!!!

Jonathan: Oh yes!

Me: Can you call?

I run down to my office and take Jonathan's call.

"Sandra, He is going to call you tomorrow," Jonathan says, pleased about how the situation is unfolding.

I'm in shock, I'm unable to speak.

"Are you there?" Jonathan asks in bewilderment.

"Yes," I say with a quiver and it's all I can push out of my mouth.

"Isn't this what you wanted?" Jonathan states, confused.

"Yes, but I assumed there would be tons of pushback. I didn't think he would be so willing to talk to me. This isn't the narrative I imagined."

When I get off the phone, I land on the floor again. My poor carpet needs to be cleaned from all the tears and black mascara.

Father reaches His hand to pull me up.

Sandra, I want to talk about why you never imagined your story unfolding like this.

"Well, because I thought I was the result of a one-night-stand so why would anyone want anything to do with me?"

And what if you are—what does that mean about who you are?

"Well, to be upfront, I feel shame. It's embarrassing. What will people think of me? Maybe I'm not as valuable."

Let's talk about this shame you haven't dealt with over your entrance into the world. When you agree with shame, you are choosing to believe the Destroyer's accusations and lies.

Throughout your life you've tried to get everything right to counter all the wrongs. I want you to know that I took your parent's shortcomings and brought something beautiful into the world. YOU.

I set you apart for wonderful things. Remember, I have waited for you for generations. There is a reason I gave you your mother's DNA and your Father's DNA. You will see it all come together. Don't let the pest make a nest in your mind. You are first and foremost MY daughter. It doesn't matter what everyone thinks or how you came into the world. I chose you and I purposefully made Myself known to you. You are known by Me!

"I love You, Father! Thank you for orchestrating this! You are right! I will not accept those lies or false identities. You are so good to me!"

The following day, May 14, 2020, I receive a text from my biological father.

> Bill Frank:
> Good afternoon Sandra,
> Last night I received a call from Jonathan. When the name Jimmy Brown and trucking was mentioned, the puzzle was complete on my end.
> I AM YOUR FATHER
> If you're not busy can you take my call?
>
> Me: Absolutely :)

Shortly after, my phone starts ringing with a New Jersey area code. This is him!

"Hello!"

"Hello Sandra! How are you doing today?"

His New Jersey accent is strong. I'm in awe—I'm talking to my biological father!

"I'm fantastic, talking to you!" This is happening! This is really happening! I think to myself.

"When I heard of Jimmy Brown, I knew you were my daughter. You see…" I'm in utter shock as he shares the story. I'm in the wonder of a moment I never imagined. I never comprehended what it would be like to talk to him and hear his voice.

Bill says, "Brown told me there was a problem but that he took care of it. I thought the pregnancy was terminated."

"So, you didn't know I existed?"

"No, I didn't. I'm telling you, had I known, things would've been different. I tell you, Sandra, it was a crazy time in my life when your mother and I were romantically involved. I'm really sorry to hear about your mother and what you've gone through. It's real unfortunate."

"Thank you for saying that."

"I actually have Will, your brother, with me in the car."

Oh wow! He already told his son. He isn't denying me! I'm floored again.

Will says in excitement, "Hey Sandra, my half-sister!"

Bill interjects, "I took the day off to recover from the shock and it's actually Will's birthday and mine today! I'm 76 and he is 23!"

"Wow, you are 76! Happy Birthday to both of you!"

"So, tell me about your family. What do you do?"

"Well, you have three grandkids! I work as an esthetician

and will be retiring after twenty years. I also JUST finished the first re-write of my book, and this happened!"

"Follow your dreams, Sand! You're not a 'should've'. Go for it!"

He's a dreamer too!

He calls me "Sand"—He gave me a nickname.

We talk for an hour. He ends the conversation with "I'm still in shock! I'll call you tomorrow. Love you."

We hang up.

"Father, my biological father said I love you. Did You hear that?! Father, how can he love me? He doesn't know me. I haven't done anything for him. He doesn't know what I have accomplished and have yet to finish. And yet, that conversation went better than I EVER could've imagined."

I like how he thinks. Sandra, authentic love is not based on merit and conditions. You don't have to fulfill a checklist, and then finally get to be in the 'loved club' There is something beautiful I want you to see. Just like he loves and accepts you immediately, so do I.

No need to perform. I love you. No need to be at Four-Wall Church every time the doors are open. I love you extravagantly anyway.

When you had children, did you not love them right away? Even in the anticipation of carrying them and then meeting them on their birthdays? He did the same thing, only 43 years later.

Champagne and gold colored confetti starts to fall from the sky. They are released with a celebratory sound. I look up to grab them as the pieces slide off my face and fill my hair. We are caught up in a whirlwind of confetti, music, and celebration.

Welcome to the party! The great cloud of witnesses has waited in great anticipation for this moment!

I see my mom, sister, a baby brother, and my grandparents

all jumping and throwing their own confetti.

I look at Father with confetti in His hair and He says, *This is worth celebrating.*

I place my hand on my heart, "I know you know how much this truly means to me. I'm at a loss for words to express the magnitude of having something I longed for turn out so amazing. May what I feel in my heart be communicated to you."

The following day, I waited for his call and it didn't happen. "Father, will he be like so many other people in my life who say they will do something and don't? I don't want that." I say in disappointment.

Sandra, you have known you existed all your life. He just found out. Give him time. He is an earthly father. He will make mistakes, he's not perfect. But I will never fail you.

"True."

I didn't bring you this far to bring disappointment. Trust Me.

The next morning, I wake up and grab my phone. Bill had sent a picture of himself earlier that morning.

In awe and wonder I declare, "Father, you did it. You did what You said You would do! You brought him to me!"

I text Bill.

> ME: Here is my favorite picture of me as a little girl and your new grandkids.
>
> Bill: That baby pic of you—that's me! LOL

Each morning, I wake up to a text from Bill.

Bill: Good morning my lovely daughter, I hope all is good in the corn fields of Iowa…

Bill: Good morning my wonderful daughter…

Bill: Good morning my precious daughter…

Bill: Good morning my beautiful daughter…

    We call or text each other almost every day. On a trip to Oklahoma we talk for hours making it one of the quickest return trips of my life. I hear stories of his childhood and how Oliver and Tessie met. Oliver was a great dancer, he won her over with his dance moves. I love to dance. I wish I could've danced with him.
    Bill says, "You would've been the apple of Tessie's eye. She always wanted a girl."
    "I wish I could've met them."
    He ends the phone call with, "Sand, you're always loved."
    "Father, Bill is so kind, and interested in my life. He actually cares about me and my family. He seems like he enjoys talking to me, and I'm not a bother. He always takes my call no matter what he is doing. He is a good communicator. He is an entrepreneur. He is friendly and enjoys laughing. His kind words and loving kindness towards me has been life changing. Do you see the words on my tears because I'm so thankful? I want to call him Dad."
    Yes, of course you do! There is a reason I picked him to be your father.
    "I would like to know. Will you tell me?"
    You needed his happy, 'no bad days' mindset to overcome what you faced as a child. After so much loss, questioning your worth,

thinking you were orphaned, I chose a man who would instantly receive you because you belong to him—and that's enough! I wired him this way. I wanted to show you what I am like through him. You don't even have to justify yourself for Me to love and accept you. I love and accept you because you belong to Me!
   I text Bill.

> Bill,
> In the couple of weeks that I've known your name, you have literally changed my life and outlook.
>
> I want to call you Dad. Would you be okay with that? I cannot tell you how your words of love and genuine kindness have left a major imprint on my heart—
>
> I will never be the same. I've NEVER felt more loved and accepted. Part of my heart grieves. I wish I had known you years ago, but in the same breath, my heart is full of gratefulness and thankfulness I finally found you!
> From your daughter who will always love you!

   We continue texting and talking on the phone for months. Covid-19 interferes with our meeting a couple of times: once on June 13, my 44th birthday, another on July 17th..
   I decide to attend a National Prayer March in Washington DC on September 26th. He decides to drive up with Candy, his wife, for the night. We arrange for the three of us to meet at a hotel.
   Twenty-five years and one day after Roy told me my mother died and I believed the lie that I would never find my biological father, I meet him for the first time.
   I anxiously wait in the hotel lobby with a couple of friends.

The elevator doors open, and I walk towards him.
"Is this the little girl that's been looking for me?"
"Yes!"
We embrace. I just got my first hug from my dad!
"I'm so glad I found you!"
"I wasn't hiding," he laughs.
"No, I guess you weren't." I agree with laughter.
We sit down for dinner. Candy shares, "I've always wanted a daughter, you can call me Mom."
"Mom it is!" I yell.
"Father, You are so redemptive! I have two parents! You truly make all things new! You've given me a whole new family!"
The waiter comes over to take our drink orders. Dad and Mom start asking about the wine list.
He notices the New Jersey accent and asks, "Where are you from?"
"New Jersey," Dad shares.
The waiter then asks us, "What is your ethnicity?" I start shaking my head in disbelief. This question follows me wherever I go! To my delight, my dad and I lock eyes and smile, and I know the answer ... because I'm sitting in the presence of my father.

Sandra and her father Bill, First Meeting
September 2020

The Great Invitation Awaits

Dear Beautiful One,

My daring hope for you after reading my adventure is you accept the Great Invitation from the Adventurer to know and experience Him.

Jesus loves you extravagantly and wants to reveal the facets of His heart to you personally.

He cares about you and what you have gone through. Before the foundation of time the Artist created you with intent and purpose.

He has amazing thoughts and wonderful plans for you!

May your walls shake down and you allow Him into your heart. May pain never separate you from His audacious love.

He is willing to remove the heart baggage so you can live fully alive. Give it to Him.

He is the ultimate Divine Exchange, Jesus' life for yours.

Cry out to Him: Jesus, I give you my heart. I want to know you and be known by you. Thank You Father God, for sending Jesus to die on the cross as me, so I can live for you! Let's start an adventure together!

You're always loved,
Sandra Rohrer

Acknowledgements

To be upfront, when God told me to finish this book, I had a BIG fit. I eventually surrendered. Thank you Jesus—for sending all of the people below to encourage me and get me to the finish line.

Encouragement is a gift and without it, these pages would be blank. I want to acknowledge my dear friends who gave me the courage to take the next step.

Josh, my husband, thank you for taking the rollercoaster ride of your life with me! You've sacrificed in supporting my dreams and I am so thankful! Can't wait to see how God rewards you. Love you!

Katherine Babcock, my number one cheerleader, undoubtedly without you walking along side me on this five-year journey, I would've quit. You believed in me and this project. You have been a blessing in my life from the first time we met at life group.

Em, my editor, you were all in! You have a special place in my heart, you helped me finish what I thought was impossible.

Acknowledgements

I couldn't have completed this without your insight and ability to pull my story out and the enormous push with the first chapters-THANK YOU!

Marian Bingaman, my mentor. You changed my life, taught me how to listen for God's voice and encounter Him. I love you and miss you!

Bill Kietzman, my Special DCI Agent, I'm already crying. The best thing to come from the death of my mother was meeting you. You have fathered me through the worst time of my life. Your level headedness and kindness towards me have proven to be life altering. Thank you!

Det. Mike Scheetz, I want to honor you and your hard work on my mother's case. Thank you for always caring about her and me! Your tenacity and relentlessness will always be remembered.

Elizabeth, my warrior mama, who taught me how to take the territory in my own heart. Who taught me what real vengeance against the Enemy of my soul looks like— and this book is it.

Shanda and Whitney, you have been friends who loved me at all times through the good, the bad, and the ugly. Your support, unrelenting prayers, and believing in me and this book have been the biggest blessings to me.

Sunny, your creativity has always inspired me, when I grow up I want to be like you.

Acknowlegements

Paula, you are a glistening gem filled with laughter and creativity. I'm so thankful for that Uber ride.

To all my mommas who have loved and nurtured me: Marian, Noreen, Melinda, Michelle, Elizabeth, Rhonda, Robin, Stephanie, Kandy, Candy, and of course my mom, Sue Kersten.

Prayer Warriors: Shanda, Noreen, Katherine B, Brittany, Melinda, Esther, Elizabeth, Tina, Elizabeth Grace, Lisa, and fellow adventurer Helen.

Recommendations:

> Counseling Resource:
> Linda Hough, a Restoring the Foundations Minister,
> www.integrated4.com
>
> Genealogy Resource:
> Eric Shubert, DNA detective, esgenealogy@outlook.com

Subscribe to Sandra's mailing list to have access to exclusive photos & content, and future KNOWN Merch at www.sandrarohrer.com

Follow Sandra on IG @sandraroars

Made in the USA
Coppell, TX
11 December 2020